Heartstrings

Heartstrings

Small Unit, Big Heart, Close-Knit

Alina Hazel

Mohammed Altaf Hussain

CONTENTS

Table of Content

Introduction

1. Introduction to the concept of a small, close-knit family.
2. Exploration of the advantages and challenges of a compact unit.
3. Setting the stage for the warmth that comes from being closely connected.

Chapter 1: "Living in Harmony"
1.1 Description of the physical space and how it fosters closeness.
1.2 Illustration of the shared daily life that contributes to intimacy.
1.3 Stories of how the family members navigate their close living quarters.

Chapter 2: "Bonding Through Everyday Moments"
2.1 Examination of the importance of mundane, everyday interactions.
2.2 Anecdotes highlighting how small, shared experiences build strong bonds.
2.3 Reflection on the significance of seemingly insignificant moments.

Chapter 3: "Roles and Responsibilities"
3.1 Discussion on how responsibilities are distributed in a small family.
3.2 Illustration of how each member's role contributes to the family dynamic.
3.3 Reflection on the balance between individuality and shared duties.

Chapter 4: "Strength in Simplicity"
4.1 Exploration of the simplicity that characterizes the family's lifestyle.
4.2 Examples of how a minimalist approach contributes to a close-knit atmosphere.
4.3 Reflection on finding strength in simplicity and shared values.

Chapter 5: "Celebrating Unity"
5.1 Showcase of the family's unique traditions and celebrations.
5.2 Highlighting the joy that comes from shared festivities.

Introduction

In the quietude of a little, unpretentious estate, the fragile dance of familial close-ness unfurls. This story leaves on an excursion through the core of a family that flourishes in the closeness of its little unit — a story woven with strings of shared spaces, ordinary minutes, and the strength that rises out of the closeness of diminutiveness. The prologue to this story is an investigation of the importance implanted in the honest magnificence of an affectionate family.

The diminutiveness of this familial unit isn't an imperative however an intentional decision — a cognizant hug of the close over the extensive. The walls of the home, however unassuming in size, exemplify an existence where every little hiding spot is pervaded with the reverberations of shared giggling, murmured discussions, and the glow of fellowship. It is inside this restricted space that the family finds the significance of closeness, where each corner turns into a phase for the unfurling show of their common lives.

The closeness of diminutiveness stretches out past the actual elements of the home; it turns into a way of thinking that shapes the family's day to day presence. The common spaces — the kitchen where smells interlace, the lounge room where stories are traded, and the rooms that hold the mysteries of dreams and goals — these become asylums of association. In the tranquil corners of their little residence, the relatives track down comfort in the effortlessness of shared residing, where the ordinary becomes unprecedented its would say.

The meaning of the closeness of diminutiveness lies an option for its to change the conventional into the remarkable. Ordinary minutes, frequently ignored in the hurrying around of bigger spaces, become the structure blocks of a rich embroidery of shared encounters. It is in the morning meals shared around a comfortable table, the nights spent in shared hushes, and the aggregate bliss in the standard that the family finds the enchantment innate in the diminutiveness of their unit.

The closeness of diminutiveness isn't a retreat from the world yet a purposeful decision to make a sanctuary — where the family can genuinely act naturally. In the peaceful and unpretentious nature of their estate, the family tracks down a shelter from the commotion and interruptions of the outer world. It is inside these walls that they can communicate weakness, celebrate triumphs, and explore the intricacies of existence without the strain to adjust to outside assumptions.

The family's hug of littleness is likewise a festival of shared liabilities and jobs. In this affectionate unit, there is an acknowledgment that every part has a fundamental impact in the familial environment. The closeness of littleness encourages a feeling of relationship, where the qualities of one supplement the shortcomings of another. It is a sensitive dance of compromise, where the aggregate prosperity outweighs individual pursuits.

As the family explores the complexities of their little unit, they find the strength that rises up out of the straightforwardness of their common presence. In this effortlessness lies a wonder that rises above the intricacies of the outside world. The common errands, the cooperative navigation, and the aggregate liability regarding the prosperity of the family become the mainstays of their solidarity. It is in the genuine idea of their common schedules that the family tracks down the versatility to endure the hardships of life.

The closeness of littleness isn't a safeguard against difficulties; rather, it turns into a wellspring of flexibility even with difficulty. When defied with difficulties, the family draws strength from their nearby bonds, exploring the challenges as a unified front. The common closeness turns into a wellspring of comfort, as every part finds backing and solace in the comprehension that they are in good company to confront life's preliminaries.

In the impression of shared liabilities and the strength brought into the world from straightforwardness, the family finds a tradition of solidarity. The diminutiveness of their unit turns into a demonstration of the getting through force of familial bonds that rise above the imperatives of actual space. The story of their common history isn't one of disengagement however a narrative of aggregate strength — a strength that is manufactured in the pot of shared minutes, difficulties, and wins.

The meaning of the closeness of diminutiveness isn't restricted to the present; it stretches out into the inheritance the family desires to leave for people in the future. In the quietude of their little residence, the family perceives that their decisions and values are forming a story that will be passed down like a loved legacy. The closeness they develop turns into a legacy — a tradition of closeness, shared liabilities, and the persevering through strength tracked down in the littleness of their familial unit.

In the bigger setting of cultural standards that frequently praise extensiveness and glory, the closeness of diminutiveness turns into a counter-story — a festival of the magnificence tracked down in straightforwardness and shared living. It challenges the thought that greater is innately better and welcomes a reconsideration of what comprises a satisfying and significant day to day life. The family's decision to embrace the closeness of littleness is a cognizant takeoff from outer assumptions, a statement that the genuine proportion of a family's abundance lies not in material belongings but rather in the profundity of their associations.

As we step into the universe of this affectionate family, the closeness of diminutiveness turns out to be in excess of a setting; it turns into a person by its own doing. It impacts the family's decisions, connections, and the manner in which they explore the excursion of coexistence. In the sections that follow, we will dig further into the lived encounters, customs, festivities, and difficulties that emerge from the closeness of littleness — a power that shapes the family's story and characterizes the significant magnificence tracked down inside the walls of their humble habitation.

1. **Introduction to the concept of a small, close-knit family.**

    In the huge embroidery of familial encounters, there exists a story that unfurls in the delicate hug of a little, affectionate family. This presentation leaves on an excursion through the core of such a nuclear family, investigating the complexities of their common presence, the bonds that integrate them, and the excellence tracked down inside the bounds of their close circle. The idea of a little, affectionate family isn't simply a primary structure; a way of thinking shapes the actual pith of their aggregate personality.

    At its center, the idea of a little, affectionate family is an intentional decision — a cognizant hug of the private over the broad. It is an acknowledgment that the strength of familial bonds frequently lies in the nature of associations as opposed to the amount of people. In this personal setting, every relative turns into a fundamental string woven into the texture of a closely knit unit, making a dynamic and interconnected entirety.

    The closeness of a little nuclear family reaches out past the actual elements of the home. It turns into a lived insight, a way of thinking that impacts the manner in which the family explores their common process. Not at all like bigger families where individual voices might mix into a whirlwind, the little, affectionate family gives a space to each voice to be heard and esteemed. It is inside this nearby circle that individual stories, dreams, and goals track down reverberation and importance.

    The thought of a little, affectionate family challenges cultural standards that frequently commend the glory of enormous families. It questions the supposition that more individuals liken to more happiness, backing, or satisfaction. All things being equal, it welcomes a reexamination of what is a significant and improving day to day life. The center movements from sheer numbers to the profundity of associations, encouraging a climate where connections are sustained with care, consideration, and a real feeling of closeness.

    The little, affectionate family isn't characterized exclusively by mathematical constraints yet by a common obligation to one another's prosperity. In this familial microcosm, the associations become significant, and the obligations are imparted to a feeling of common comprehension.

The relatives, however very few, make an emotionally supportive network that is powerful and strong, secured in the conviction that the strength of the unit lies in its solidarity and common perspective.

Inside the idea of a little, affectionate family, the actual space they possess isn't simply a house; it is a safe-haven of shared encounters. The home turns into an observer to the giggling, tears, and development of every relative. Its walls reverberation with the accounts of shared feasts, murmured discussions, and the ordinary minutes that characterize the cadence of day to day life. The house isn't simply a haven yet a residing demonstration of the bonds that make the family's presence really private.

In the effortlessness of their common presence, the family finds a marvel that rises above the intricacies of the outer world. Regular schedules, little tokens of care, and the delight found in unremarkable minutes become the structure blocks of their common account. It is in the genuine idea of their regular routines that the relatives track down a wellspring of satisfaction, satisfaction, and a common personality that is produced in the cauldron of their affectionate unit.

The idea of a little, affectionate family is likewise reflected in the manner in which they explore jobs and obligations. In this personal setting, there is an acknowledgment that every part assumes a crucial part in the working of the family. There is a sensitive dance of shared obligations and cooperative independent direction, where the qualities of one supplement the shortcomings of another. The obligations are not weights to be carried independently; all things considered, they become strings that weave an embroidery of common help and relationship.

Not at all like bigger families where jobs might be more specific, the little, affectionate family frequently encounters a smoothness in obligations. Every part wears numerous caps, adding to different parts of day to day life. This common methodology encourages a feeling of solidarity as well as considers a more profound comprehension of one another's commitments and difficulties. It is inside this common scene of jobs and obligations that the family finds a strength that emerges from their aggregate endeavors.

The meaning of a little, affectionate family is additionally featured in snapshots of festivity and difficulty. In the midst of delight, the closeness enhances the common bliss, transforming standard occasions into exceptional festivals. Whether it be birthday events, accomplishments, or basic triumphs, the affectionate family tracks down happiness in the common experience, making enduring recollections that become valued achievements in their aggregate process.

Essentially, in snapshots of misfortune, the closeness turns into a wellspring of solidarity. When confronted with difficulties, the relatives draw upon their nearby bonds, offering help and comfort to each other. The common encounters and history become an establishment whereupon they stand strong despite life's vulnerabilities. The solidarity manufactured inside the little, affectionate family turns into a safeguard that shields them from the tempests of life.

The idea of a little, affectionate family isn't invulnerable to the intricacies of human connections. Clashes, conflicts, and varying points of view might emerge, yet it is inside the closeness of their unit that the family learns the craft of correspondence, split the difference, and pardoning. The closeness turns into a stage for fair discussions and an eagerness to explore moves with a common obligation to understanding and development.

As the family explores the excursion of life inside the structure of their little, affectionate unit, they additionally perceive the significance of inheritance. Their decisions, the qualities they maintain, and the associations they support are commitments to an inheritance that rises above individual lifetimes. The idea of a little, affectionate family becomes a current reality as well as a gift went down through ages — a legacy of closeness, mutual perspective, and persevering through bonds.

In the more extensive cultural setting, the idea of a little, affectionate family challenges the common story that outcome in day to day life is inseparable from sheer numbers. It offers an elective point of view — one that underscores the profundity of associations over the expansiveness of connections. The family's decision to focus on closeness turns into an unobtrusive disobedience to outer tensions, a statement that the extravagance of their familial life isn't estimated by cultural assumptions however by the significance of their common encounters.

As we drench ourselves in the investigation of the idea of a little, affectionate family, it becomes clear that this isn't simply a primary decision; it is a lifestyle. The closeness, shared liabilities, and flexibility become strings that weave a story wealthy in importance and reason. In the parts that follow, we will dig further into the lived encounters, customs, festivities, and difficulties that emerge from the idea of a little, affectionate family — an idea that changes the standard into the remarkable inside the walls of their valued dwelling place.

2. **Exploration of the advantages and challenges of a compact unit.**

Inside the limits of a reduced familial unit lies a rich embroidery woven with the two benefits and difficulties — a fragile interchange that shapes the elements of a little, affectionate family. This investigation dives into the nuanced features of their common presence, revealing insight into the qualities that rise out of closeness as well as the obstacles that accompany exploring the complexities of life inside a minimal unit.

Benefits:

Closeness and Solid Bonds:

One of the premier benefits of a smaller familial unit is the closeness that normally blooms inside its limits. The nearness of relatives encourages compelling close to home bonds, taking into consideration more profound associations and understanding.

In the more modest setting, every part turns into a basic piece of the day to day account, sharing encounters, dreams, and difficulties. This closeness frequently brings about a familial brotherhood that is hard to recreate in bigger settings.

Compelling Correspondence:

The conservative idea of a little family works with more successful and direct correspondence. With less people to explore, it becomes simpler for relatives to offer their viewpoints, sentiments, and concerns. This immediate correspondence advances a culture of transparency, where each voice is heard and esteemed. The clearness in correspondence is a strong resource, adding to an amicable climate where false impressions are limited.

Shared Liabilities:

In a conservative familial unit, the dissemination of obligations will in general be all the more equally spread among relatives. The more modest number of people requires a cooperative way to deal with everyday errands and tasks. This common obligation encourages a feeling of solidarity as well as guarantees that every part effectively adds to the working of the family. The family turns into a strong group, cooperating towards shared objectives.

Productivity and Adaptability:

The productivity of navigation and the adaptability in adjusting to changing conditions are remarkable benefits in a conservative family. With less people included, choices can be made all the more quickly, permitting the family to answer speedily to developing circumstances. The adaptability to adjust plans, oblige individual necessities, and turn notwithstanding difficulties turns out to be more open inside the smoothed out construction of a little familial unit.

Closer Emotionally supportive network:

The conservativeness of the nuclear family frequently means a more prompt and open emotionally supportive network. Whether praising accomplishments or exploring troublesome times, relatives are genuinely and sincerely more like each other. This vicinity encourages an encouraging group of people that is promptly accessible, making a feeling of safety and consolation. The family turns into a safe-haven where people can rest on each other during both glad and testing minutes.

Challenges:

Restricted Variety of Points of view:

While the closeness of a little, affectionate family is a benefit, it can likewise introduce a test with regards to a restricted variety of points of view. With less people, there might be a smaller scope of encounters, suppositions, and perspectives inside the familial unit. This might possibly prompt carefully protected area elements, where the family's aggregate viewpoint is less shifted contrasted with bigger, more assorted settings.

Potential for Over-Contribution:

The closeness inside a minimal familial unit may, on occasion, lead to over-contribution in one another's lives. While a strong climate is useful, an overabundance of contribution may unintentionally encroach on individual independence and security. Finding some kind of harmony among help and permitting space for self-awareness and autonomy becomes significant in moderating this test.

Restricted Assets and Aptitude:

A little family might confront impediments concerning the two assets and mastery. Monetary assets, for instance, might be more compelled in a minimized unit, influencing the family's capacity to explore specific difficulties. Likewise, the broadness of mastery inside the family might be smaller, prompting a dependence on outside hotspots for particular information or abilities. Finding savvy fixes and utilizing outside assets become fundamental in tending to these limits.

Potential for Strengthened Clashes:

The closeness inside a little family can enhance the effect of contentions. Conflicts or strains might be felt all the more intensely, given the nearness of relatives. Settling clashes successfully becomes basic to keep an amicable climate. Techniques for open correspondence, undivided attention, and compromise are critical devices in alleviating the potential for heightened clashes inside the smaller unit.

Hazard of Overburdening Shared Liabilities:

While shared liabilities are a benefit, there is a gamble of overburdening specific relatives, especially on the off chance that the obligations are not conveyed even-handedly. In a little unit, every part's commitment conveys critical weight, and a lopsided dispersion of errands might prompt sensations of hatred or burn-out. A scrupulous way to deal with adjusting liabilities and guaranteeing a fair circulation becomes fundamental to relieve this test.

Exploring the Equilibrium:

The benefits and difficulties innate in a conservative familial unit highlight the requirement for a sensitive equilibrium in exploring the complexities of shared living. The strength of a little, affectionate family lies in its capacity to use the benefits while proactively tending to the difficulties. A few procedures add to keeping up with this harmony and guaranteeing a flourishing relational intricacy:

Developing Open Correspondence:

To moderate the potential for clashes and guarantee powerful independent direction, open correspondence is central. Making a culture of straightforwardness, where relatives feel open to offering their viewpoints and sentiments, cultivates a better climate. Customary family gatherings, where concerns and thoughts are shared straightforwardly, add to the general prosperity of the smaller unit.

Cultivating Individual Independence:

Perceiving and regarding individual independence is essential in forestalling over-contribution and permitting relatives the space to seek after self-awareness. Empowering every part to seek after their inclinations, side interests, and yearnings freely adds to a balanced familial unit. Offsetting fellowship with individual pursuits guarantees an agreeable mix of shared encounters and individual independence.

Broadening Points of view:

While a little family may innately have less different points of view, purposeful endeavors can be made to expand the scope of encounters. Drawing in with outer networks, partaking in social or local area occasions, and encouraging associations past the familial unit add to an additional differed and enhanced point of view. Embracing variety, even external the family, balances the potential for insularity.

Fair Dissemination of Obligations:

Keeping away from the traps of overburdening explicit relatives requires a faithful way to deal with the circulation of obligations. Consistently surveying and rethinking errands, recognizing individual qualities and inclinations, and guaranteeing reasonableness in the division of work add to a more adjusted dynamic. The objective is to establish a climate where every part feels esteemed and their commitments are perceived.

Looking for Outside Assets and Backing:

Recognizing the constraints innate in a little unit, the family can effectively look for outside assets and backing when required. Whether it's getting to proficient ability, taking part in local area projects, or looking for exhortation from outside sources, the family can use outer organizations to supplement their inner assets. This approach improves the family's flexibility and strength notwithstanding challenges.

Observing Individual and Aggregate Accomplishments:

Perceiving and celebrating both individual and aggregate accomplishments adds to a positive family culture. Every part's victories, regardless of how little, are recognized and celebrated, cultivating a deep satisfaction and support. All the while, aggregate accomplishments, for example, defeating difficulties or arriving at shared objectives, reinforce the familial bond. Adjusting the acknowledgment of individual achievements with an aggregate pride improves the general relational intricacy.

Generally, exploring the benefits and difficulties of a minimized familial unit requires a nuanced approach that recognizes the exceptional elements at play.

The family's capacity to proactively address difficulties, exploit their assets, and adjust to developing conditions adds to the versatility and energy of their common presence.

The little, affectionate family, when aware of its elements, turns into a microcosm of help, understanding, and getting through association inside the more extensive material of familial encounters.

3. **Setting the stage for the warmth that comes from being closely connected.**

In the domain of familial connections, there exists a special and significant warmth that exudes from being firmly associated — a glow that rises above actual vicinity and reverberates in the common encounters, giggling, and cozy minutes inside an affectionate family. This investigation tries to make way for this glow, diving into the layers of profound wealth, shared stories, and the profound feeling of having a place that characterize the pith of firmly associated families.

The Heartbeat of Harmony:

At the center of the glow in firmly associated families lies the heartbeat of harmony — a musicality that ties relatives in an amicable dance of shared encounters. A glow exudes from the basic yet significant demonstration of being available for each other. Amidst the rushing about of day to day existence, this harmony turns into a safe-haven — a space where people track down comfort, support, and a feeling of having a place.

The glow of fellowship isn't exclusively bound to excellent motions or elaborate festivals; rather, it flourishes in the normal minutes that characterize the texture of day to day life. It is in the common morning meals, the unconstrained discussions, and the calm nights spent in one another's organization that the heartbeat of fellowship turns out to be generally unmistakable. In these ordinary cooperations, relatives make a mosaic of shared recollections that adds to the glow encompassing the familial unit.

Shared Accounts and Stories:

Firmly associated families are narrators, winding around an embroidery of shared stories that resound across ages. These accounts, frequently passed down from seniors to the more youthful individuals, become the soul that courses through the family's veins. They are more than simple tales; they are the aggregate memory and character of the familial unit, adding to the glow that comes from knowing one's underlying foundations.

The common stories envelop a range of stories — from the silly ventures of the past to the victories and difficulties that molded the family's excursion. In the retelling of these accounts, whether around the supper table or during extraordinary get-togethers, relatives find an association with an option that could be bigger than themselves. It is through these common stories that the glow of inheritance, custom, and a common history is encouraged, making a feeling of progression and having a place.

An Ensemble of Giggling and Euphoria:

Giggling, similar to a melodic orchestra, reverberates inside firmly associated families, turning into a sign of the glow they share. It is the unconstrained ejections of shared humor, within jokes, and the irresistible chuckling that penetrate the familial space. Chuckling fills in as a limiting power, fashioning associations that go indeed and laying out a happy air where bliss turns into an aggregate encounter.

The glow of chuckling isn't restricted to snapshots of festivity; it is interlaced into the texture of regular daily existence. Whether enduring difficulties or praising triumphs, firmly associated families track down comfort and strength in shared chuckling. It turns into a language of own — a general articulation rises above contrasts and builds up the familial bond. The reverberations of giggling resound through the passages of the family's common spaces, establishing a climate where satisfaction is definitely not a detached feeling yet an aggregate festival.

The Specialty of Presence:

In firmly associated families, the specialty of presence outweighs amazing signals. It is the straightforward demonstration of being there for each other, offering a listening ear, a consoling hug, or a consoling grin. The glow got from this presence isn't dependent upon luxurious presentations of fondness however flourishes in the nuances of veritable consideration and mindfulness.

The specialty of presence is exemplified in snapshots of weakness and strength the same. In the midst of distress, a firmly associated family comes together for the one out of luck, offering quiet help and understanding. Alternately, during snapshots of win, the common happiness is amplified as relatives revel in one another's achievements. The craft of presence turns into a quiet certification — a demonstration of the steady help that characterizes the firmly associated familial bond.

Making Customs of Association:

Firmly associated families frequently make customs — revered customs that act as anchors in the back and forth movement of life. These customs, whether day to day, week by week, or attached to critical achievements, become holy snapshots of association. They are the family suppers where discussions stream uninhibitedly, the film evenings that inspire shared chuckling, or the yearly practices that mark the progression of time.

Customs of association add to the glow inside the family by cultivating a feeling of congruity and consistency. They become customs not simply in their reiteration but rather in the close to home reverberation they convey. In these common ceremonies, relatives discover a feeling of safety, realizing that these snapshots of association are constants in the steadily changing scene of life.

Developing Bonds Through Shared Difficulties:

The glow inside firmly associated families isn't invulnerable to the difficulties life presents. As a matter of fact, it is during seasons of difficulty that the familial bonds develop and the glow turns into a wellspring of versatility. Shared difficulties — be they outside emergencies or unseen fits of turmoil — act as pots that test and reinforce the familial associations.

Confronting difficulties together, firmly associated families draw upon the aggregate strength got from their bonds. The common obligation to help each other through various challenges turns into a mainstay of the familial warmth. It is in the aggregate defeating of deterrents that the relatives produce a more profound comprehension of one another's assets, weaknesses, and the steady help that characterizes their firmly associated unit.

Having a place and Character:

The glow inside firmly associated families stretches out to the significant feeling of having a place and personality that rises out of shared roots. It is the information that one is essential for an option that could be more significant than oneself — a heredity, an inheritance, and a familial personality that rises above independence. This feeling of having a place is a wellspring of solace, establishing relatives in a common story that gives importance to their reality.

In firmly associated families, the glow of having a place isn't restrictive; it is comprehensive and inviting. New individuals who join through marriage or different associations are embraced into the overlay, improving the familial personality. The glow extends to wrap all who become piece of the firmly associated unit, making a feeling of inclusivity that reinforces the bonds much further.

The Implicit Language of Adoration:

Inside the firmly associated family, love turns into an implicit language — a quiet yet strong power that saturates each communication. It is communicated in the delicate motions, the strong looks, and the common quiets that say a lot. Love turns into the propensity that streams underneath the outer layer of day to day existence, restricting relatives in an embroidery woven with strings of care, warmth, and understanding.

This implicit language of affection isn't bound to fantastic statements; present in the customary minutes accentuate day to day life. It is the demonstration of setting up a most loved feast, offering a consoling touch during troublesome times, or essentially sharing a calm second together. The glow got from this implicit language of affection is persevering, making a groundwork of safety and profound association inside the firmly associated family.

Encouraging Flexibility and Versatility:

The glow inside firmly associated families adds to their strength and versatility notwithstanding life's vulnerabilities. The bonds fashioned through shared encounters, chuckling, and challenges become a wellspring of solidarity during seasons of progress.

Firmly associated families explore the exciting bends in the road of existence with an aggregate soul that emerges from their close associations.

The capacity to adjust to changing conditions is improved by the glow of familial help. Whether it be a migration, a lifelong shift, or other huge life altering events, the firmly associated family finds comfort in the information that they face these changes as a unified front. The glow turns into a directing light, enlightening the way ahead and imparting a feeling of trust notwithstanding the unexplored world.

Embracing the Multi-layered Nature of Warmth:

The glow inside firmly associated families is multi-layered, embracing both the light and shadowed parts of life. It's anything but a particular feeling however a range that incorporates bliss, distress, versatility, and development. In snapshots of festivity, the glow turns into a bubbly gleam, enlightening the familial space with shared satisfaction. On the other hand, in the midst of distress, it changes into an encouraging hug, offering comfort and a feeling of shared trouble.

The complex idea of warmth likewise reaches out to the development and advancement of the familial bonds over the long haul. As relatives explore the different phases of life, the glow adjusts and develops, reflecting the consistently changing scene of individual and aggregate encounters. It is a no nonsense substance that flourishes with the lavishness of the family's excursion — an excursion set apart by achievements, challenges, and the unfaltering help that characterizes firmly associated families.

The Ceremonies of Association as Anchors:

The ceremonies of association inside firmly associated families act as anchors in the rhythmic movement of life, establishing relatives from a common perspective of congruity. These ceremonies, whether established in social practices, strict practices, or just family-explicit traditions, make a musical rhythm that adds to the glow of the familial unit. They become ageless minutes where the family meets up to celebrate, reflect, and fortify their associations.

In investigating these customs, we uncover the importance they hold in cultivating a feeling of character and mutual perspective. Whether it's the yearly occasion get-togethers, the week by week family suppers, or the unique functions that mark huge life altering situations, these customs become touchpoints that anchor the family in an aggregate story. They are not only occasions on the schedule; they are articulations of adoration, having a place, and the persevering through warmth that rises above the limits of time.

The Craft of Adjusting Freedom and Reliance:

Inside firmly associated families, the craft of offsetting individual freedom with aggregate relationship turns into a vital part of supporting warmth.

While the nuclear family flourishes with shared encounters and common help, it likewise perceives the significance of individual development, independence, and the quest for individual goals. It is a sensitive balance where the qualities of the individual add to the strength of the entirety.

Empowering individual freedom doesn't decrease the glow inside the firmly associated family; rather, it enhances it. Every relative's novel process, accomplishments, and self-improvement become strings that upgrade the familial woven artwork. The glow is supported not through smothering consistency but rather through the festival of different singularity inside the steady hug of the familial unit.

The Tradition of Warmth:

As firmly associated families cross the embroidery of time, they abandon a heritage — a heritage not estimated in material riches but rather in the glow of connections, shared esteems, and persevering through associations. This heritage turns into a gift went down through ages, molding the familial character and filling in as a directing light for the people who come later. It is a demonstration of the strength, versatility, and cherish that characterize the firmly associated unit.

The tradition of warmth reaches out past the actual family, impacting the networks and social orders where these families are inserted. Firmly associated families, with their accentuation on fellowship, support, and shared values, add to the more extensive texture of social agreement. They become reference points of warmth, emanating a positive impact that stretches out a long ways past the limits of their close familial circle.

In making way for the investigation of the glow that comes from being firmly associated, we observe that this glow is certainly not a static or transient inclination. It is a living, developing power that winds through the day to day routines, shared encounters, and ceremonies of association inside firmly associated families. The complex idea of warmth embraces bliss and distress, development and versatility, making a rich embroidery that characterizes the quintessence of familial bonds.

As we venture further into the core of familial connections, we will disentangle the complexities of this glow — looking at the ceremonies that anchor it, the fragile harmony among autonomy and reliance, and the getting through heritage that it abandons. It is a festival of the magnificence found inside the firmly associated unit, an investigation of the manners by which warmth shapes the story of everyday life, and an affirmation of the significant effect firmly associated families have on the more extensive social texture.

Chapter 1

"Living in Harmony"

Living as one isn't simply a method of presence; a significant way of thinking reaches out to each feature of our lives, changing the everyday into an ensemble of equilibrium and concurrence. At its center, living together as one suggests a profound association with oneself, with others, and with the normal world, encouraging a feeling of solidarity that rises above individual limits.

The excursion to living as one starts inside, with a careful investigation of one's viewpoints, feelings, and values. It is tied in with developing mindfulness and embracing a comprehensive way to deal with individual prosperity. In this internal scene, people endeavor to accomplish an agreeable harmony between their physical, mental, and profound aspects. Practices like contemplation, care, and self-reflection become fundamental devices in this excursion, directing people to a condition of internal harmony and balance.

Reaching out past oneself, living as one includes building significant associations with others. Networks flourish when they are established on standards of sympathy, participation, and shared regard. In an agreeable local area, variety is praised, and people meet up to make an embroidery of shared encounters.

Open correspondence, undivided attention, and a certifiable comprehension of one another's points of view structure the mainstays of agreeable connections, encouraging a climate where everybody feels esteemed and upheld.

Living as one likewise envelops a significant association with the normal world. It is an acknowledgment of the relationship among people and the climate, with a promise to manageable practices and natural obligation. Agreeable living includes valuing the excellence of nature, grasping its cycles, and proceeding with caution on the Earth. This association with the normal world advances ecological stewardship as well as sustains a feeling of wonderment and appreciation for the planet we call home.

With regards to day to day life, residing as one includes establishing a sustaining and strong climate where every part can flourish. It is tied in with cultivating solid securities, viable correspondence, and a common feeling of direction. Amicable families focus on quality time, shared understanding, and the aggregate quest for joy. In such families, clashes are drawn closer with persistence and sympathy, and goals look to reinforce the nuclear family as opposed to plant disagreement.

Working environments that embrace the way of thinking of living together as one are portrayed by a positive and comprehensive culture. Workers feel enabled, heard, and esteemed for their commitments. Administration is established in standards of decency and straightforwardness, advancing a feeling of solidarity and shared objectives. In an amicable workplace, imagination prospers, joint effort flourishes, and people track down satisfaction in proficient accomplishments as well as in the feeling of having a place with an aggregate undertaking.

Residing as one reaches out to cultural designs, where equity, fairness, and inclusivity are vital. It requires an aggregate obligation to tending to foundational disparities and making an existence where each individual has the potential chance to thrive. Amicable social orders focus on the prosperity of every one of their individuals, esteeming social union and the benefit of all over individual interests. In such social orders, variety isn't just recognized however celebrated as a wellspring of solidarity and flexibility.

On a worldwide scale, living as one suggests a common obligation regarding the prosperity of the whole planet. It calls for global collaboration in resolving major problems, for example, environmental change, neediness, and medical services. In an amicable world, countries team up to find supportable arrangements, perceiving that the difficulties we face rise above borders and require aggregate activity.

The idea of living together as one is well established in antiquated methods of reasoning and shrewdness customs.

Numerous native societies have long figured out the interconnectedness of all things and have lived together as one with nature for ages. In the cutting edge setting, this shrewdness takes on recharged importance as people and social orders wrestle with the results of quick mechanical progressions, ecological corruption, and the quest for realism to the detriment of prosperity.

Living as one is a comprehensive and extraordinary way to deal with life that includes oneself, connections, networks, and the world in general. A way of thinking welcomes people to investigate their inward scenes, construct significant associations with others, and cultivate a profound association with the normal world. In this present reality where dissension and division frequently rule features, residing together as one fills in as a reference point, directing us toward a future where equilibrium, sympathy, and solidarity win.

1.1 Description of the physical space and how it fosters closeness.

The actual space wherein people collaborate assumes a urgent part in molding the elements of connections and encouraging a feeling of closeness. Whether it's a home, a work environment, or a local area setting, the plan and design of the climate significantly influence the manner in which individuals interface and draw in with each other. In this investigation of actual space and its job in encouraging closeness, we dig into different viewpoints that add to a feeling of solidarity, shared encounters, and interconnectedness.

At the core of any affectionate space is an insightfully planned mutual region. These spaces act as the focal point of social cooperations, giving a stage to people to meet up, share encounters, and fabricate associations. A comfortable parlor with open to seating, an enticing kitchen where fragrances of shared feasts wait, or a collective nursery washed in normal light — this large number of components add to a warm and inviting climate. These public regions are not simply practical spaces; they are purposeful plans that energize inhabitants or local area individuals to assemble, chat, and structure bonds that reach out past the bounds of their singular living spaces.

Building subtleties likewise assume a huge part in forming the closeness inside an actual space. Open floor plans, for example, separate customary boundaries, making ease between various regions. This plan supports normal development and associations, permitting individuals to flawlessly progress starting with one space then onto the next. The shortfall of unbending divisions cultivates a feeling of harmony, as people can participate in discussions and exercises without feeling truly detached. Essentially, shared offices like common kitchens, game rooms, or wellness focuses add to a feeling of brotherhood by giving spaces where occupants can take part in shared exercises and leisure activities.

The plan of living spaces inside a local area or a structure likewise impacts social elements. Vicinity matters, and while living quarters are planned in bunches as opposed to detached units, occupants are bound to naturally cooperate.

Passages become roads for chance experiences, and shared doorways set out open doors for easygoing discussions. The actual design, thusly, turns into a quiet facilitator of associations, encouraging a feeling of commonality and friendliness that rises above simple vicinity.

The consolidation of nature into the actual space further improves the feeling of closeness. Green spaces, whether they are local area nurseries, yards, or parks, furnish inhabitants with a common safe-haven. The presence of nature adds stylish allure as well as offers a background for collective exercises. Occupants might meet up for cultivating projects, open air yoga meetings, or essentially to partake in the serenity of nature. This common association with the regular habitat makes a security among local area individuals, encouraging a feeling of stewardship for the space they by and large occupy.

Shared conveniences and offices inside an actual space contribute essentially to the formation of an affectionate local area. Offices, for example, public venues, libraries, or collaborating spaces become centers of connection. They offer occupants chances to take part in shared exercises, from book clubs to cooperative work projects. These common spaces are utilitarian as well as act as central places where people with different foundations and interests merge, making a rich embroidery of encounters and viewpoints.

The plan of private living spaces likewise assumes a part in cultivating closeness. While mutual regions unite individuals, the security and solace of individual living spaces are similarly significant. Smart plan in individual units, like open overhangs, enormous windows that welcome normal light, and adaptable designs that oblige different ways of life, adds to the general prosperity of occupants. At the point when individuals feel good and happy in their own spaces, they are bound to connect emphatically with the more extensive local area.

The consolidation of social components inside the actual space adds a layer of wealth to the public experience. Whether it's common fine art, social images, or assigned spaces for social exercises, these components make a feeling of personality and having a place. Social variety isn't simply recognized however celebrated, enhancing the collective texture with a heap of customs, customs, and stories. This deliberate consolidation of social components cultivates a comprehensive climate where everybody feels a deep satisfaction in their legacy and an oddity to find out about the foundations of their neighbors.

Innovation, when incorporated flawlessly, can likewise add to closeness inside an actual space. Savvy innovations that work with correspondence, shared schedules, or local area gatherings furnish inhabitants with instruments to associate and arrange easily. From coordinating occasions to tending to public worries, these innovative combinations span holes and improve the general feeling of local area.

Virtual spaces supplement actual ones, permitting occupants to remain associated in any event, when they are not truly present in collective regions.

A vital part of cultivating closeness inside an actual space is the purposeful production of chances for shared encounters. Local area occasions, studios, and festivities unite inhabitants, giving roads to communication past day to day schedules. Whether it's a potluck supper, a social celebration, or a cooperative workmanship project, these common encounters make enduring recollections and fortify the securities inside the local area. The actual space, hence, ought to be versatile to oblige different exercises, guaranteeing that occupants can effectively take part in the common existence of the space.

The job of style ought not be disregarded while thinking about the effect of actual space on closeness. Smart plan, satisfying style, and an amicable variety range add to a positive and welcoming environment. Feel go past simple visual allure; they summon feelings and make a feeling of solace. At the point when people feel a deep satisfaction in their common environmental elements, it improves their association with the local area, encouraging an aggregate liability regarding the upkeep and prosperity of the actual space.

Adaptability in the utilization of room is one more key consider encouraging closeness. Spaces that can adjust to various requirements and exercises permit occupants to customize their connections. A multipurpose room, for instance, can change from a yoga studio to a gathering space, obliging an assortment of local area exercises. This adaptability urges occupants to effectively shape the common space in light of their developing necessities and interests, cultivating a feeling of pride and strengthening.

Developing the subject of the actual space's part in encouraging closeness, it's fundamental to dig into the mental and profound effect of plan decisions. The game plan of furniture, the utilization of varieties, and the general feel of a space can fundamentally impact the mind-set and communications of its inhabitants. In a space planned with deliberateness, occupants feel a feeling of solace, security, and having a place, factors that are instrumental in developing an affectionate local area.

The design of common spaces inside an actual climate is essential in forming social elements. Consider an open kitchen plan in a shared living space; it fills its useful need as well as turns into a locus for casual get-togethers and extemporaneous discussions. The spatial game plan empowers a characteristic progression of collaborations, killing actual boundaries and cultivating a feeling of receptiveness. Also, guest plans in mutual regions, whether in shared nurseries or familiar rooms, can be decisively situated to work with eye to eye discussions, establishing a climate helpful for certified associations.

Lighting, both normal and fake, is a strong component in establishing the vibe of an actual space. Sufficiently bright regions add to a positive and welcoming air, advancing a feeling of warmth and friendliness. Huge windows that permit adequate normal light to channel through establish an association with the outside climate, getting the outside and upgrading the general prosperity of the occupants. Nicely positioned counterfeit lighting, in the interim, can make comfortable niches for cozy discussions or dynamic spaces for local area occasions, adding layers to the shared insight.

The utilization of variety brain science is another perspective that fundamentally impacts the close to home tone of an actual space. Warm tones like gritty earthy colors and delicate yellows can inspire sensations of solace and brotherhood, while cool tones like blues and greens can make a feeling of quiet and serenity. The cautious choice of varieties in collective regions can bring out unambiguous feelings, adding to a general good and agreeable climate. An even variety range can likewise mirror the social variety inside a local area, making a space that resounds with the fluctuated foundations of its occupants.

Spatial acoustics assume a frequently misjudged part in cultivating closeness inside an actual climate. The plan ought to represent sound levels and acoustics to guarantee that mutual regions are helpful for both lively gathering exercises and calm, intelligent minutes. The cautious situation of acoustic boards, the selection of materials that assimilate or reflect sound, and the making of assigned spaces for different commotion levels all add to a climate where people can associate through both enthusiastic discussions and tranquil thought.

The consolidation of craftsmanship and plan components inside an actual space adds layers of significance and works with a feeling of shared character. Wall paintings, models, and other imaginative articulations act as central focuses that inhabitants can accumulate around, appreciate, and talk about. These components become visual markers of the local area's set of experiences, values, and yearnings, making a common story that ties people together. The deliberate incorporation of nearby workmanship and specialty can additionally build up a feeling of spot, interfacing the local area to its social roots.

Adaptability in the plan of collective spaces is fundamental to oblige the advancing necessities of the local area. Versatile spaces that can be reconfigured for various exercises guarantee that the actual climate stays dynamic and responsive. Moveable furnishings, particular designs, and multipurpose rooms permit inhabitants to shape their common spaces in light of the necessities existing apart from everything else, whether it's a local area occasion, a calm understanding space, or a cooperative work-space. This adaptability enables occupants to take part in the co-formation of their mutual climate effectively.

Biophilic plan, which coordinates normal components into the fabricated climate, adds to a feeling of prosperity and association. Integrating plants, green walls, or water highlights into collective spaces adds stylish allure as well as improves inhabitants' association with nature.

Biophilic configuration has been connected to further developed mind-set, dimin-ished feelings of anxiety, and expanded mental capability, factors that emphatically impact social communications and connections inside a local area. An actual space planned in light of biophilia turns into a safe-haven that sustains both individual and aggregate prosperity.

The idea of "third spaces" inside a local area further underlines the significance of casual get-together spots. Past confidential homes and formal collective regions, third spaces are casual gathering places where inhabitants can suddenly meet up. These can be seats in a yard, a common device shed, or a local area notice board. These spots sup-port chance experiences, improvised discussions, and the development of associations that go past arranged occasions. The formation of these casual get-together focuses adds to the natural improvement of closeness inside a local area.

Supportability is a critical part of present day local area plan and adds to the general prosperity of the inhabitants. A reasonable actual climate, whether through energy-effective highlights, squander decrease drives, or green structure rehearses, encourages a common obligation to ecological stewardship. Occupants of a local area with a practical ethos frequently share a feeling of obligation for the planet, making a bind-ing together bond that reaches out past relational associations. Feasible practices can likewise be woven into common exercises, for example, local area gardens, fertilizing the soil drives, or sustainable power projects, further reinforcing the feeling of mutual perspective.

The versatility of an actual space to oblige different ages is essential for making a comprehensive and intergenerational local area. Insightful plan thinks about the necessities of youngsters, grown-ups, and seniors, guaranteeing that collective spaces are available and inviting to people, everything being equal. Play regions for youngsters, seating choices for more established occupants, and spaces that take special care of the assorted interests of various age bunches add to a local area where everybody feels esteemed and included.

In the advanced age, the reconciliation of innovation into the actual space can improve availability and correspondence. Savvy home elements, local area applications, and divided advanced stages smooth out correspondence between occupants, making it more straightforward to arrange occasions, share assets, and remain informed about local area news. The consistent coordination of innovation into the actual space guarantees that occupants can use computerized devices to upgrade their collective experience without forfeiting the individual and human parts of association.

The actual space wherein people live and connect is a material that, when mindfully planned, can turn into an impetus for encouraging closeness inside a local area. From the format of common regions to the joining of normal components, the plan decisions add to the general feel and elements of connections.

The mental and close to home effect of spatial plan, combined with deliberate components like craftsmanship, adaptability, and supportability, establishes an actual climate that goes past usefulness to shape the social texture of a local area effectively. As people explore through these mindfully planned spaces, they track down a spot to dwell as well as a material whereupon the craft of association, shared encounters, and public closeness is persistently painted.

1.2 Illustration of the shared daily life that contributes to intimacy.

In the embroidery of public living, the strings of shared day to day existence complicatedly wind around together to make a rich and close texture of associations. The rhythms of day to day existence inside an affectionate local area are an orchestra of shared encounters, cooperative endeavors, and the unobtrusive subtleties that structure the premise of persevering through connections. From dawn to nightfall, the public routine turns into a material where inhabitants paint their accounts, share their delights and difficulties, and on the whole add to the lively mosaic of shared presence.

Mornings in an affectionate local area unfurl with a novel mix of individual customs and collective commitment. As the sun rises, occupants might end up attracted to shared spaces like collective kitchens or yards, where the fragrance of blending espresso blends with the hints of good tidings and chuckling. Morning strolls or public activity meetings become open doors for relaxed experiences, encouraging associations that reach out past the shallow. The common beginning to the day establishes an inspirational vibe, making a feeling of solidarity that waves through the local area.

The demonstration of fellowshipping together is a foundation of shared day to day existence inside an affectionate local area. Whether it's a mutual breakfast in a common kitchen or a potluck supper in a collective eating region, feasts become shared occasions that go past simple sustenance. Inhabitants accumulate to share recipes, trade culinary tips, and bond over an affection for food. These common dinners become spaces for social trade, where various cooking styles mirror the rich embroidered artwork of the local area's experiences, cultivating an appreciation for one another's practices.

Work areas inside the local area become centers of cooperation and common help. Whether people telecommute or share a collaborating space, the everyday schedule includes a mix of centered work and unconstrained connections. Shared work areas give open doors to inhabitants to team up on projects, look for input, or essentially share a snapshot of brotherhood during a short breather. The lines among expert and individual life obscure in these spaces, establishing a climate where occupants can draw on one another's abilities and aptitude.

Kids playing in collective regions add a happy and dynamic component to day to day existence. Jungle gyms, stops, or shared gardens become stages where the giggling of kids resounds, making an energetic setting to day to day existence. The common obligation of paying special attention to each other's kids cultivates a feeling of more distant family, where neighbors become proxy aunties, uncles, and grandparents. The public spaces become stages for both arranged and unconstrained playdates, support-ing the social improvement of the local area's most youthful individuals.

Day to day errands take on a collective aspect, changing routine undertakings into shared liabilities. Whether it's watching out for a local area garden, coordinating reus-ing drives, or taking part in a local cleanup, occupants unite to add to the prosperity of their common climate. The demonstration of working next to each other in these collective endeavors not just encourages a feeling of satisfaction in the common space yet in addition fortifies the securities among local area individuals. The ordinary becomes significant when people team up to make a spotless, green, and very much kept up with living climate.

Shared festivals and achievements intersperse the day to day daily schedule, making snapshots of aggregate bliss and reflection. Birthday celebrations, commemorations, and social celebrations become events for common get-togethers. The public spaces change into scenes for celebrations, where embellishments, music, and shared dinners become the scenery for aggregate cheer. These festivals act as touchpoints locally's common history, making a feeling of progression and association across ages.

The everyday beat additionally incorporates snapshots of calm reflection and shared care. Mutual spaces might have contemplation meetings, yoga classes, or calm understanding corners, furnishing inhabitants with open doors for reflection and unwinding. The deliberate joining of spaces for quietness inside the everyday schedule recognizes the significance of mental prosperity and encourages a feeling of aggregate care.

Shared transportation and portability arrangements add to the interconnectedness of day to day existence. Carpooling, shared bikes, or mutual electric bikes become pragmatic arrangements as well as roads for easygoing discussions and shared ventures. The common obligation of decreasing the local area's carbon impression turns into an aggregate responsibility, making a feeling of ecological stewardship that saturates day to day existence.

Nights in an affectionate local area carry a characteristic rhythm to shared day to day existence. Shared suppers, whether coordinated or off the cuff, become events for occupants to meet up and loosen up. Shared spaces change into comfortable corners where stories are traded, thoughts are discussed, and kinships extend. The public air urges occupants to relinquish the burdens of the day, establishing a climate where authentic associations can thrive.

Far-reaching developments and imaginative articulations become basic to the everyday existence of an affectionate local area. Whether it's a local area workmanship display, a verse perusing, or a music practice in a collective space, occupants effectively add to the social dynamic quality of the local area. The festival of innovativeness turns into a common undertaking, with people displaying their gifts and everybody valuing the different articulations inside the local area.

Shared liabilities stretch out to the really focusing on pets inside the local area. Canine strolling turns, mutual pet consideration drives, and assigned pet-accommodating regions make a feeling of shared liability regarding the fuzzy individuals from the local area. Pets become allies for individual occupants as well as impetuses for unconstrained cooperations and shared snapshots of happiness.

Day to day schedules likewise incorporate snapshots of unconstrained association and unrehearsed get-togethers. Whether it's a neighbor dropping by for a fast visit, an off the cuff game night in a common space, or a common film screening, the day to day schedule is sprinkled with snapshots of spontaneous association. These unconstrained communications add a layer of eccentricism to day to day existence, setting out open doors for occupants to produce securities past planned occasions.

In the midst of challenge or emergency, the closeness of the local area radiates through in shared help and strength. Whether it's mobilizing together to help a neighbor confronting trouble, coordinating common assets during crises, or offering profound help during difficult stretches, the texture of closeness woven through day to day existence turns into a wellspring of solidarity. The common encounters, both upbeat and testing, add to the flexibility and cohesiveness of the local area.

The interconnectedness of day to day existence reaches out to shared independent direction and administration inside the local area. Occupants effectively partake in local gatherings, contribute thoughts to dynamic cycles, and team up on drives that shape the aggregate future. The feeling of pride and shared liability regarding the local area's prosperity encourages a culture of dynamic citizenship and cooperation.

Inside the common everyday existence of an affectionate local area, the idea of shared care and backing arises as a focal topic. The everyday collaborations, whether arranged or unconstrained, are mixed with a feeling of certifiable worry for the prosperity of individual occupants. This ethos of common consideration stretches out past the reasonable items of mutual living and turns into an essential piece of the local area's character.

Shared childcare obligations weave an organization of help among guardians inside the local area.

Whether it's getting sorted out playgroups, keeping an eye on, or public after-school exercises, guardians find comfort in the information that their youngsters are encircled by an organization of caring people. The common obligation regarding childcare eases up the singular weights as well as makes a feeling of more distant family, where the aggregate prosperity of kids is a common need.

Shared wellbeing and health drives become an aggregate pursuit. Shared practice classes, wellbeing studios, and gathering exercises like climbing or trekking make a culture of focusing on wellbeing. Occupants move and persuade one another, framing a local area where people feel upheld in their own wellbeing processes. The common obligation to prosperity cultivates a feeling of responsibility and support, making a good gradually expanding influence inside the local area.

Encouraging groups of people for the older individuals from the local area become a fundamental part of shared day to day existence. Whether through coordinated exercises, normal registrations, or help with everyday errands, inhabitants meet up to guarantee the prosperity of their more established neighbors. The mutual spaces become regions where the insight and encounters of seniors are esteemed, making an intergenerational security that improves the everyday texture of the local area.

Shared assets and cooperative drives add to a feeling of financial fortitude. Whether it's mass purchasing, collective planting for shared produce, or ability sharing for monetary undertakings, the local area effectively takes part in rehearses that advance financial flexibility. The common help in the midst of monetary test and the festival of aggregate monetary accomplishments make a feeling of reliance that rises above individual monetary limits.

Day to day existence in an affectionate local area is set apart by a culture of open correspondence and compromise. Ordinary local gatherings, shared dynamic cycles, and the accessibility of collective spaces for exchange establish a climate where clashes are tended to transparently and helpfully. Inhabitants feel engaged to voice concerns, and the common obligation to settling issues cultivates a climate of shared understanding and development.

The festival of variety inside the local area isn't simply a latent affirmation however a functioning hug in day to day existence. Social trade occasions, language classes, and shared customs become indispensable parts of the day to day everyday practice. The purposeful festival of assorted foundations makes a comprehensive environment where inhabitants value the lavishness that alternate points of view bring to their mutual experience.

Cooperative imaginative ventures and social drives become a common articulation of inventiveness. Whether it's a local area wall painting, a cooperative craftsmanship presentation, or a social exhibition in a mutual space, occupants effectively add to the imaginative and social embroidery of the local area. The common appreciation for inventiveness turns into a wellspring of motivation and association, cultivating a feeling of aggregate personality.

Day to day existence in an affectionate local area likewise includes shared mastering and expertise improvement. Occupants offer studios, share mastery, and participate in common learning drives. The mutual spaces change into centers of information trade, where people contribute their abilities as well as effectively look for open doors for individual and aggregate development.

The reconciliation of innovation into day to day existence works with consistent correspondence and network. Shared computerized stages, local area discussions, and shrewd advancements inside common spaces upgrade the straightforwardness with which occupants stay associated. Whether for coordinating occasions, sharing assets, or essentially encouraging a feeling of virtual local area, innovation turns into a device that supplements the human-driven parts of public living.

Shared transportation arrangements contribute not exclusively to ecological manageability yet additionally to day to day associations. Carpooling, bicycle sharing, or common electric vehicles set out open doors for occupants to associate during day to day drives. The common excursion turns into a similitude for the aggregate way the local area crosses, cultivating a feeling of harmony even in the basic demonstration of voyaging.

The day to day everyday practice in an affectionate local area is interspersed by shared customs that extend the feeling of association. Whether it's a week after week local area feast, a month to month book club, or an occasional celebration festivity, these customs become secures locally's common schedule. Occupants anticipate these minutes, and the expectation constructs a feeling of coherence and shared personality.

In the midst of emergency, the versatility of the local area turns out to be most apparent in shared encouraging groups of people. Whether it's revitalizing together during catastrophic events, wellbeing crises, or individual difficulties, inhabitants effectively add to one another's prosperity. The common reaction to provokes turns into a demonstration of the strength of the securities framed in day to day existence, displaying the local area's ability to weather conditions storms together.

The ethos of shared care stretches out to the encouraging of a feeling of having a place for newbies. Inviting boards of trustees, mentorship programs, and public occasions explicitly intended for new inhabitants make a smooth reconciliation process.

The day to day collaborations, whether in common spaces or during shared exercises, become open doors for rookies to feel at ease inside the local area rapidly.

The common everyday existence of an affectionate local area isn't simply a grouping of routine exercises; it is an aggregate orchestra of care, support, and shared encounters. From the viable parts of childcare and wellbeing drives to the profound components of open correspondence and social festivals, each aspect of day to day existence adds to the closeness inside the local area. It is inside the embroidery of these common minutes, customs, and connections that the genuine substance of closeness is woven, making a living story that mirrors the magnificence of public living. The common regular routine turns into a demonstration of the strength of human associations, the flexibility of the local area, and the wealth that comes from effectively partaking in the common excursion of public presence.

1.3 Stories of how the family members navigate their close living quarters.

Inside the affectionate hug of shared living spaces, the tales of relatives exploring their regular routines unfurl with an embroidery of shared encounters, difficulties, and snapshots of association. Every family, a microcosm inside the more extensive local area, winds around its one of a kind story, mixing the unremarkable with the phenomenal in the personal setting of close living quarters. These accounts offer looks into the elements of familial connections, the versatility expected in collective living, and the excellence that arises when people meet up in shared spaces.

In the core of these common living quarters, morning schedules become an orchestra of composed exercises. Guardians shuffle restroom plans, youngsters rush to prepare for school, and public kitchens witness a movement of breakfast arrangements. The closeness of residing spaces requires a degree of synchronization, where relatives figure out how to move agreeably inside the common climate. These wake-up routines become snapshots of shared readiness, establishing the vibe for the day ahead and encouraging a feeling of public beat.

Shared responsibilities regarding family tasks become a critical part of day to day daily routine inside close experiencing quarters. The division of errands reaches out past individual families to public spaces, making a feeling of aggregate stewardship. Families cooperate to keep up with neatness, request, and usefulness in shared regions. From clearing shared lobbies to taking part in area cleaning drives, the common obligation regarding the actual climate turns into a holding action that cultivates a feeling of local area pride.

Youngsters, in the nearness of public spaces, track down the two close companions and a feeling of more distant family. Playdates in shared gardens or mutual play regions become a typical event.

The chuckling of kids turns into a soundtrack that resonates through the nearby living quarters, making an energetic and dynamic environment. The common obligation regarding watching out for each other's kids turns into a shared standard, making an organization of help that rises above individual families.

Dinner times inside close living quarters change into mutual occasions, mirroring the social variety inside the local area. Families accumulate in common eating regions or shared kitchens, sharing recipes, culinary customs, and the delight of fellowshipping together. The rich embroidery of foundations inside the local area is reflected in the range of cooking styles that effortlessness shared tables. These common dinners become sustenance for the body as well as a festival of variety and a stage for social trade.

Relational peculiarities inside close living quarters are molded by the transaction of individual and collective spaces. While private living spaces offer asylums for isolation and individual reflection, collective regions become stages for shared exercises and associations. Families explore the fragile harmony between cultivating individual protection and effectively taking part in the public existence of shared spaces. The flexibility of relatives to moving between these circles adds to the general congruity inside close living quarters.

The reconciliation of innovation into everyday day to day daily routine inside shared experiencing spaces turns into an instrument for association and correspondence. Whether through local area discussions, shared advanced schedules, or shrewd home innovations, families influence innovation to upgrade their network. Virtual spaces supplement the actual ones, giving stages to arranging occasions, sharing assets, and remaining informed about local area news. The consistent coordination of innovation turns into an extension that interfaces families inside their families as well as with the more extensive local area.

Relatives explore the common work areas inside close living quarters, obscuring the lines among expert and individual life. Whether it's folks telecommuting or cooperative activities inside collaborating spaces, families wind up working one next to the other with neighbors. The common workplace turns into an impetus for proficient systems administration, expertise sharing, and the cross-fertilization of thoughts. Families figure out how to make a harmony between centered work and unconstrained collaborations, adding to a dynamic expert local area.

Shared transportation arrangements influence family versatility inside close living quarters. Carpooling, common bikes, or shared electric bikes become down to earth answers for everyday driving. Families coordinate transportation plans, making an organization of shared portability that reaches out past individual families. The common excursion becomes a method for arriving at objections as well as a chance for families to interface during everyday drives.

Family festivities inside close living quarters are set apart by a mix of individual and common celebrations. Whether it's a birthday celebration in a common space, a commemoration festivity in a common nursery, or a social celebration noticed on the whole, families add to the general environment of satisfaction and merriment inside the local area. The consistent progress between confidential festivals and public occasions mirrors the versatility and inclusivity imbued in everyday daily routine inside close experiencing quarters.

The common social and creative articulations inside the local area become roads for family cooperation and commitment. Families feature their imaginative abilities in cooperative workmanship projects, social exhibitions, and local area occasions. Kids, enlivened by the creative undertakings around them, effectively take part in studios and displays. The mutual spaces become exhibitions for familial innovativeness, encouraging a feeling of satisfaction and shared character.

In the midst of challenge or emergency, the versatility of families inside close living quarters becomes obvious in shared encouraging groups of people. Whether confronting wellbeing crises, individual difficulties, or unanticipated conditions, families effectively add to the prosperity of their neighbors. The common encounters of euphoria and challenge become strings that reinforce the securities inside the local area, making a wellbeing net that rises above individual families.

Novices to the local area explore the reconciliation cycle fully supported by families inside close living quarters. Inviting panels, friendly signals, and collective occasions intended for novices work with a smooth digestion into the affectionate climate. Families take on mentorship jobs, sharing bits of knowledge about common life and effectively including rookies in the common encounters that characterize local area living.

Relatives take part in common dynamic cycles that shape the aggregate future inside close living quarters. Whether through dynamic support in local gatherings, contributing plans to shared drives, or teaming up on area projects, families assume an imperative part in molding the public story. The feeling of pride and shared liability reaches out past individual families, making a culture of dynamic citizenship inside the local area.

The coordination of reasonable practices inside everyday life adds to the by and large ecological awareness of close living quarters. Whether through shared reusing drives, local area nurseries, or energy-productive practices inside families, families effectively add to the maintainability of the collective climate. The common obligation to eco-accommodating living turns into a common worth that saturates day to day existence.

Relatives take part in the persistent course of shared mastering and ability advancement inside close living quarters.

Whether through coordinated studios, collective learning drives, or ability sharing stages, families effectively add to the way of life of information trade. The public spaces become center points of shared mastery, cultivating a climate where learning turns into an aggregate undertaking.

As the sun sets and the mutual spaces change, nights in close living quarters unfurl with a remarkable mix of shared exercises, family time, and local area commitment. These hours become a material whereupon families paint their accounts, making an embroidery of shared minutes, discussions, and the excellence of aggregate residing.

Collective suppers become a focal point of night everyday routine inside close experiencing quarters. Families assemble in shared kitchens or public feasting regions, adding to the vivacious murmur of discussions and the ringing of utensils. The climate is rich with the smells of assorted cooking styles, mirroring the differed foundations of families inside the local area. These mutual suppers are tied in with sustaining the body as well as feeding the feeling of local area, as families meet up to share stories, giggling, and the delights of a good to go feast.

The mutual spaces take on another life at night, becoming comfortable corners for shared exercises. Families assemble for table games, film evenings, or offhand narrating meetings in shared lounges. The common spaces become expansions of individual families, cultivating an environment where families can consistently progress among private and public exercises. The chuckling and brotherhood that occupy these spaces make a feeling of warmth and harmony.

Comprehensive developments inside the local area frequently track down their stage during the night hours. Families effectively partake in putting together and going to social exhibitions, craftsmanship displays, or verse readings in shared spaces. These occasions become events for families to grandstand their social lavishness, adding energy to the local area's common story. The nights become a period for appreciation and festivity of the variety that characterizes close living quarters.

Shared liabilities stretch out to night errands, where families add to the upkeep of collective spaces. Whether it's alternating to clean shared regions or taking part in neighborhood upkeep drives, families effectively take part in the collective every-day practice. The night tasks become open doors for families to team up, making a common feeling of satisfaction in the tidiness and efficiency of the local area.

Youngsters' sleep time schedules in close living quarters frequently include a common feeling of local area. Public storytimes, evening walks around shared yards, or the aggregate management of open air play make a steady organization for families with small kids. The sleep time customs become snapshots of shared nurturing, where the local area effectively takes part in establishing a safe and sustaining climate for its most youthful individuals.

The nights additionally witness the incorporation of innovation into day to day everyday routine inside close experiencing quarters. Whether it's families streaming motion pictures together, captivating in virtual get-togethers, or basically associating with neighbors through computerized stages, innovation turns into a device for both unwinding and local area building. The consistent change among physical and virtual spaces improves the network that characterizes the nights in close living quarters.

Evening strolls in shared green spaces become a well known movement for families inside close living quarters. The quietness of public gardens or stops gives a back-ground to families to loosen up, interface, and partake in the magnificence of nature. These strolls become snapshots of reflection and association, encouraging a feeling of peacefulness that rises above individual families.

In the midst of festivity or accomplishment, families inside close living quarters meet up for public merriments. Whether it's a graduation, an achievement birthday, or an individual accomplishment, families effectively participate in sorting out and partaking in shared festivals. The common spaces change into scenes for shared euphoria, where the achievements of one family become a wellspring of festivity for the whole local area.

Relatives frequently take part in collective leisure activities or shared vested parties during the night hours. Whether it's a book club, a planting club, or a common leisure activity space inside the local area, families track down roads to seek after normal interests. These common exercises become stages for holding, learning, and associating with neighbors who share comparable interests.

The night schedule additionally incorporates snapshots of calm reflection and unwinding inside close living quarters. Public spaces might have contemplation meetings, yoga classes, or calm perusing corners where families can loosen up. These snapshots of serenity become basic to the general prosperity of families, making a harmony between the dynamic quality of collective life and the requirement for individual restoration.

Relatives frequently expand solicitations for night social occasions or off the cuff parties inside close living quarters. Whether it's a straightforward casual get-together, a common grill in public spaces, or a cooperative cooking meeting, families effectively add to the social texture of the local area. The nights become open doors for unconstrained associations and the manufacturing of new fellowships.

Nights in close living quarters frequently witness the mixing of individual and mutual festivals. Whether it's a family praising a unique event or a local area wide occasion, the limits among private and shared celebrations obscure. Families effectively add to the happy climate, establishing a climate where individual bliss becomes interlaced with the aggregate prosperity.

The ethos of common consideration reaches out to nights, where families effectively take part in shared encouraging groups of people. Whether giving help during testing times, offering a listening ear, or coordinating shared drives to help neighbors, families assume an essential part in making a steady local area. The nights become a period for communicating sympathy, empathy, and the fortitude that characterizes close living quarters.

Rookies to the local area frequently track down their underlying associations during night get-togethers or occasions. Families inside close living quarters broaden solicitations, participate in discussions, and effectively include newbies in the common exercises that characterize evening life. The nights become a door for novices to incorporate into the texture of the local area, making a feeling of having a place all along.

The tales of relatives exploring their nearby residing quarters reach out into the nights, where the elements of collective residing keep on unfurling. Whether through shared dinners, widespread developments, or unrehearsed get-togethers, the nights become a material whereupon families add to the common story of local area life. In this personal setting, the obligations of family reach out past the walls of private living spaces, entwining with the more extensive woven artwork of shared presence inside close living quarters.

Chapter 2

"Bonding Through Everyday Moments"

In the complicated woven artwork of human connections, frequently the strings of ordinary minutes weave the most grounded bonds. These conventional, yet significantly critical, examples shape the texture of our associations with others. Whether it's the common chuckling over morning espresso, the soothing quietness of a night walk, or the cooperative exertion in setting up a dinner, these regular minutes become the paste that ties people together in the mosaic of life. As we investigate the topic of "Holding Through Regular Minutes," we dive into the magnificence and profundity that dwells in the effortlessness of shared encounters.

Wake-up routines become sacrosanct snapshots of association inside the embroidery of daily existence. As the sun rises, families stir to the mood of another day. Shared spaces like kitchens and public nurseries become the background for morning schedules, where people and families participate in exercises that set the vibe for the hours to come. The fragrance of newly fermented espresso drifts through the air, blending with the hints of delicate good tidings and the stirring of papers. These basic yet significant minutes become a common encounter that encourages a feeling of harmony, making an establishment for the day's unfurling story.

Collective feasts rise above simple food; they become shared functions of association. Whether it's a family supper or a local potluck, the demonstration of sharing a feast reaches out past the sustenance of the body. In the planning and happiness regarding food, people figure out something worth agreeing on where social variety is commended, and individual stories are shared. The feasting table changes into a space where chuckling, discussion, and the ringing of utensils become the language of association. These regular feasts, whether arranged or unconstrained, add to the fortifying of familial and common bonds.

The common obligations of day to day errands mesh a feeling of participation and cooperation into the texture of day to day existence. Whether it's keeping an eye on a collective nursery, partaking in neighborhood cleanup drives, or just alternating to keep up with shared spaces, people meet up in the standard undertakings that maintain their living climate. These common obligations not just add to the actual prosperity of the local area yet additionally develop a feeling of participation, imparting a deep satisfaction in on the whole focusing on the spaces they possess.

Youngsters playing in public regions mix daily existence with the delight and immediacy of energetic energy. Jungle gyms, stops, or shared yards become stages where kids investigate, learn, and structure bonds that frequently rise above the limits of their nearby families. The giggling of kids turns into a soundtrack that jazzes up the local area, making a lively air where the common obligation regarding their prosperity encourages a feeling of more distant family among neighbors.

The night schedule unfurls as a material for shared exercises and family time. As the sun sets, collective spaces change into comfortable corners where families participate in prepackaged games, film evenings, or unrehearsed narrating meetings. The common residing regions become augmentations of individual families, cultivating an environment where the lines among private and collective exercises obscure. These nights become snapshots of association, unwinding, and the production of shared recollections.

Widespread developments inside the local area frequently track down their stage during the night hours. Families effectively partake in arranging and going to social exhibitions, workmanship displays, or verse readings in public spaces. These occasions become events for families to grandstand their social wealth, adding liveliness to the local area's common story. The nights become a period for appreciation and festivity of the variety that characterizes close living quarters.

Shared transportation arrangements influence the texture of regular day to day existence, setting out open doors for association during day to day drives. Carpooling, mutual bikes, or shared electric bikes become pragmatic answers for everyday transportation needs.

The common excursion becomes a method for arriving at objections as well as a chance for unconstrained associations and the fashioning of connections. The basic demonstration of driving turns into a common encounter that adds to the interconnectedness of people inside the local area.

Nights in close living quarters frequently witness the mixing of individual and collective festivals. Whether it's a family commending an exceptional event or a local area wide occasion, the limits among private and shared celebrations obscure. Families effectively add to the blissful air, establishing a climate where individual joy becomes interlaced with the aggregate prosperity. These festivals become strings that weave an embroidery of shared delight, reinforcing the securities that interface people inside the local area.

The ethos of common consideration stretches out to nights, where families effectively take part in shared encouraging groups of people. Whether giving help during testing times, offering a listening ear, or sorting out mutual drives to help neighbors, families assume a critical part in making a steady local area. The nights become a period for communicating sympathy, empathy, and the fortitude that characterizes close living quarters.

Relatives frequently broaden solicitations for night social events or improvised parties inside close living quarters. Whether it's a basic casual get-together, a common grill in mutual spaces, or a cooperative cooking meeting, families effectively add to the social texture of the local area. The nights become open doors for unconstrained associations and the fashioning of new fellowships.

The night schedule additionally incorporates snapshots of calm reflection and unwinding inside close living quarters. Collective spaces might have reflection meetings, yoga classes, or calm perusing corners where families can loosen up. These snapshots of quietness become essential to the general prosperity of families, making a harmony between the dynamic quality of collective life and the requirement for individual revival.

In the midst of festivity or accomplishment, families inside close living quarters meet up for common celebrations. Whether it's a graduation, an achievement birthday, or an individual accomplishment, families effectively take part in sorting out and taking part in common festivals. The mutual spaces change into settings for shared happiness, where the achievements of one family become a wellspring of festivity for the whole local area.

Rookies to the local area explore the coordination interaction fully supported by families inside close living quarters. Inviting councils, friendly signals, and common occasions intended for novices work with a smooth digestion into the affectionate climate. Families take on mentorship jobs, sharing bits of knowledge about collective life and effectively including rookies in the common encounters that characterize local area living.

Relatives participate in mutual dynamic cycles that shape the aggregate future inside close living quarters. Whether through dynamic cooperation in local gatherings, contributing plans to shared drives, or teaming up on area projects, families assume an essential part in molding the collective story. The feeling of pride and shared liability reaches out past individual families, making a culture of dynamic citizenship inside the local area.

The joining of supportable practices inside day to day life adds to the generally natural cognizance of close living quarters. Whether through shared reusing drives, local area nurseries, or energy-effective practices inside families, families effectively add to the maintainability of the collective climate. The common obligation to eco-accommodating living turns into a common worth that pervades day to day existence.

Relatives participate in the persistent course of shared acquiring and ability advancement inside close living quarters. Whether through coordinated studios, collective learning drives, or ability sharing stages, families effectively add to the way of life of information trade. The common spaces become center points of shared mastery, encouraging a climate where learning turns into an aggregate undertaking.

As the day unfurls into the material of night inside close living quarters, the many-sided dance of shared encounters keeps on winding around the texture of association. The enchantment of holding through ordinary minutes arrives at its peak in the peacefulness of common spaces and the glow of familial associations. These minutes, apparently customary yet significantly effective, rise above the everyday practice and become the pith of mutual living.

Evening strolls in shared green spaces become a well known movement for families inside close living quarters. The tranquility of collective gardens or stops gives a scenery to families to loosen up, interface, and partake in the excellence of nature. These strolls become snapshots of reflection and association, cultivating a feeling of peacefulness that rises above individual families. As families wander through these public spaces, the night air conveys with it the murmur of shared stories, chuckling, and the stir of leaves, making an air of harmony and fellowship.

In the midst of festivity or accomplishment, families inside close living quarters meet up for mutual merriments. Whether it's a graduation, an achievement birthday, or an individual accomplishment, families effectively participate in sorting out and taking part in shared festivals. The public spaces change into settings for shared bliss, where the achievements of one family become a wellspring of festivity for the whole local area. These common festivals become snapshots of individual victory as well as strings that tight spot families and neighbors in an aggregate embroidery of joy and shared accomplishment.

Relatives frequently participate in public leisure activities or shared vested parties during the night hours. Whether it's a book club, a cultivating club, or a common side interest space inside the local area, families track down roads to seek after normal interests. These common exercises become stages for holding, learning, and associating with neighbors who share comparative interests. The mutual spaces become energetic with the aggregate energy of families meeting up to investigate and support shared side interests, encouraging a feeling of local area inside individual pursuits.

The night schedule likewise incorporates snapshots of calm reflection and unwinding inside close living quarters. Common spaces might have contemplation meetings, yoga classes, or calm perusing corners where families can loosen up. These snapshots of serenity become essential to the general prosperity of families, making a harmony between the dynamic quality of shared life and the requirement for individual revival. As families find comfort in these common spaces of quiet, the mutual environment turns into a wellspring of both individual thoughtfulness and aggregate tranquility.

Relatives frequently broaden solicitations for night social affairs or off the cuff parties inside close living quarters. Whether it's a basic casual get-together, a common grill in public spaces, or a cooperative cooking meeting, families effectively add to the social texture of the local area. The nights become open doors for unconstrained associations and the fashioning of new kinships. These extemporaneous get-togethers mirror the soul of transparency and brotherhood that characterizes close residing quarters, where families embrace the immediacy of association in ordinary communications.

Nights in close living quarters frequently witness the mixing of individual and shared festivals. Whether it's a family praising a unique event or a local area wide occasion, the limits among private and shared celebrations obscure. Families effectively add to the euphoric air, establishing a climate where individual satisfaction becomes interwoven with the aggregate prosperity. These festivals become strings that weave an embroidery of shared bliss, reinforcing the securities that interface people inside the local area.

The ethos of common consideration reaches out to nights, where families effectively take part in shared encouraging groups of people. Whether giving help during testing times, offering a listening ear, or sorting out mutual drives to help neighbors, families assume a significant part in making a strong local area. The nights become a period for communicating sympathy, empathy, and the fortitude that characterizes close living quarters.

Rookies to the local area explore the combination cycle fully supported by families inside close living quarters. Inviting boards of trustees, friendly motions, and common occasions intended for rookies work with a smooth digestion into the affectionate climate. Families take on mentorship jobs, sharing bits of knowledge about mutual life and effectively including newbies in the common encounters that characterize local area living.

The nights become a period for producing associations, as families expand tokens of neighborliness and consideration, causing rookies to feel invited as well as embraced by the glow of collective living.

Relatives participate in mutual dynamic cycles that shape the aggregate future inside close living quarters. Whether through dynamic support in local gatherings, contributing plans to shared drives, or teaming up on area projects, families assume an imperative part in molding the collective story. The feeling of pride and shared liability stretches out past individual families, making a culture of dynamic citizenship inside the local area. Nights become fields for helpful exchange, aggregate navigation, and the supporting of a common vision for what's in store.

The joining of manageable practices inside day to day life adds to the generally ecological awareness of close living quarters. Whether through shared reusing drives, local area nurseries, or energy-proficient practices inside families, families effectively add to the supportability of the mutual climate. The common obligation to eco-accommodating living turns into a common worth that penetrates day to day existence. As families partake in public endeavors towards natural stewardship, the nights become snapshots of aggregate liability, where the common objective of safeguarding the climate entwines with the texture of local area residing.

Relatives take part in the consistent course of shared mastering and ability improvement inside close living quarters. Whether through coordinated studios, mutual learning drives, or expertise sharing stages, families effectively add to the way of life of information trade. The public spaces become centers of shared mastery, encouraging a climate where learning turns into an aggregate undertaking. Nights become open doors for families to participate in scholarly pursuits, extend their ranges of abilities, and effectively partake in the development of a culture of shared information inside the local area.

As the night unfurls inside close living quarters, the exchange of shared minutes, familial associations, and collective commitment lays out a picture of regular day to day existence that is rich with profundity and importance. It is at these times, whether everyday or unprecedented, that the genuine excellence of common living arises. Families explore the sensitive harmony among individual and shared encounters, adding to the orchestra of associations that characterize the pith of affectionate networks. The nights become a material where the brushstrokes of regular minutes, shared chuckling, and aggregate festivals consolidate to make a show-stopper of human association and shared presence.

2.1 Examination of the importance of mundane, everyday interactions.

In the complex woven artwork of human association, the strings of ordinary collaborations structure the actual texture of our social presence. Frequently eclipsed by additional earth shattering occasions, these unremarkable experiences hold a remarkable importance in molding connections, encouraging local area bonds, and impacting the general nature of our lives.

In this investigation, we leave on an excursion to look at the significant significance of commonplace, ordinary communications, disentangling the layers that add to the lavishness of human association.

At the core of ordinary associations lie the underpinnings of social bonds and connections. These are the apparently normal minutes that come to pass over a day — easygoing good tidings, shared grins, brief discussions — that on the whole weave the complicated snare of human association. Inside these apparently standard trades trust is constructed, commonality is sustained, and the underlying foundations of significant connections grab hold. The significance of these cooperations lies not in their pomposity but rather in their consistency, filling in as the paste that ties people in the embroidery of local area and shared insight.

Everyday connections act as the money of social union inside networks. In shared living spaces, neighborhoods, or working environments, the day to day trade of merriments, gestures of affirmation, and brief talks in mutual regions adds to the feeling of having a place and interconnectedness. These communications make a social environment where people feel seen, recognized, and coordinated into the bigger social texture. It is through these little, steady signals that the ethos of local area is supported, rising above the person to frame an aggregate character.

The work environment, specifically, is a pot for the significance of unremarkable collaborations. Past the customs of gatherings and organized joint efforts, the water-cooler discussions, shared snacks, and passing welcomes in the corridor assume a significant part in molding the hierarchical culture. These apparently unnoticeable minutes cultivate fellowship, separate various leveled obstructions, and add to a positive workplace. The aggregate state of mind, resolve, and generally speaking elements inside a work environment are fundamentally impacted by the nature of ordinary collaborations among partners.

Inside families, commonplace collaborations structure the bedrock of closeness and familial bonds. It is in the common minutes around the morning meal table, the relaxed trades during family suppers, or the giggling over trivial issues that the profound closeness inside a family is sustained. These communications, frequently excused as normal, convey the heaviness of shared history, inside jokes, and a feeling of having a place. In the back and forth movement of day to day existence, families manufacture a profound association through the consistency and consistency of these unremarkable yet significant minutes.

The area, as a microcosm of local area living, blossoms with ordinary communications. Whether it's the friendly wave across the wall, improvised visits during a night walk, or shared liabilities like area watch or public upkeep, the significance of these regular communications is highlighted in the production of a steady and closely knit local area. In close living quarters, the day to day trades add to a feeling of shared liability, security, and the comprehension that one isn't just an occupant however an essential piece of a public embroidery.

Commonplace connections go about as an impetus for separating social obstructions and cultivating inclusivity. In a world that frequently wrestles with divisions in view of race, orientation, financial status, or social contrasts, the meaning of regular connections turns out to be considerably more articulated. A straightforward grin, a cordial hello, or a common snapshot of giggling has the ability to rise above cultural partitions, making spans between people who could somehow see themselves as various. These little motions prepare for a more comprehensive and amicable social texture.

Ordinary communications add to the profound prosperity of people. The total impact of positive, confirming, and strong communications in day to day existence assumes a critical part in forming one's psychological and close to home scene. Be it the inspiring discussions with partners, the glow of familial trades, or the friendly signals inside a local area, these communications become a wellspring of close to home sustenance. On the other hand, the nonattendance or negative nature of regular associations can affect emotional wellness, featuring the significant impact these apparently unremarkable minutes hold over our general prosperity.

The meaning of everyday communications is obvious in the computerized age. While innovation has changed the manner in which we convey, the embodiment of ordinary connections stays as pivotal as could be expected. Web-based entertainment stages, informing applications, and virtual associations supplement however don't supplant the worth of up close and personal or even voice-to-voice connections. In a period where computerized correspondence is unavoidable, the yearning for legitimate, face to face trades highlights the inborn significance of these regular minutes in keeping up with veritable associations.

Everyday communications add to the social wealth of networks. It is inside the easygoing discussions, shared customs, and the passing down of social tales that the character of a local area is shaped. The social embroidery is woven through the everyday communications that reflect shared values, customs, and the aggregate memory of a gathering. The significance of saving and praising these regular trades lies in the progression and advancement of social legacy inside networks.

In instructive settings, commonplace connections shape the learning climate and understudy prosperity. Past conventional homeroom guidance, the trades between understudies, educators, and staff individuals make the environment of a learning local area. Whether it's the common minutes during breaks, the consolation from educators, or the help from peers, these connections add to a positive instructive encounter. The profound associations shaped through ordinary communications in schools lastingly affect understudies' scholastic presentation and in general turn of events.

The expanding influence of positive ordinary communications stretches out to more extensive cultural effects. In a world wrestling with issues of disruptiveness, segregation, and disconnection, the combined effect of little, positive trades isn't to be undervalued. Thoughtful gestures, articulations of sympathy, and the affirmation of shared mankind in regular collaborations add to the making of a more empathetic and grasping society. The significance of these collaborations becomes apparent in the potential they hold to cultivate positive cultural change.

Everyday communications are the structure blocks of versatility despite difficulty. In testing times, be it individual emergencies, local area wide difficulties, or worldwide pandemics, the strength of regular associations turns into a wellspring of comfort and backing. Whether it's the neighbor checking in, the colleague offering support, or the relative giving a listening ear, these regular collaborations become life savers that assist people and networks explore misfortune with more noteworthy strength.

The purposeful development of positive ordinary collaborations is a pathway to self-awareness. Cognizant endeavors to participate in significant discussions, offer thanks, and cultivate positive associations in day to day existence add to one's capacity to understand anyone on a deeper level and relational abilities. The familiarity with the significance of these minutes permits people to effectively partake in establishing a positive social climate, for themselves as well as for everyone around them.

Commonplace associations add to the advancement of sympathy and understanding. At the point when people participate in regular collaborations that include undivided attention, open correspondence, and a certifiable interest in others, they add to the improvement of sympathy. Figuring out the viewpoints, encounters, and feelings of everyone around us throughout day to day existence assembles extensions of association and destroys obstructions of bias and misjudging.

The significant significance of commonplace, ordinary cooperations stretches out past the quick effect on people and networks, venturing into the domains of self-improvement, cultural elements, and the actual texture of human life.

Ordinary collaborations act as an establishment for the improvement of the capacity to understand people on a deeper level. In the embroidery of day to day existence, people explore a range of feelings, from delight and energy to dissatisfaction and disillusionment. Regular connections give a setting to understanding and dealing with these feelings, both inside oneself and corresponding to other people. The capacity to communicate feelings legitimately, identify with the sensations of others, and explore relational elements is sharpened through the consistent act of ordinary connections. This capacity to understand people on a deeper level, developed through the commonplace, turns into an important resource in private and expert circles.

The nature of regular cooperations straightforwardly impacts the general prosperity of people. Research in brain science reliably highlights the effect of positive social associations on mental and close to home wellbeing. Day to day dosages of giggling, shared snapshots of delight, and the solace got from routine trades add to a feeling of satisfaction and bliss. On the other hand, an absence of good connections or continuous pessimistic experiences can prompt sensations of disengagement, stress, and lessened prosperity. In this way, the meaning of regular connections becomes central in encouraging a positive mental and close to home scene.

Commonplace cooperations assume a urgent part in the development of recollections and shared stories. It is inside the apparently standard discussions, shared jokes, and routine trades that the accounts of our lives are composed. These minutes, frequently disregarded in their effortlessness, amass to frame the sections of individual and common accounts. Whether it's the describing of an entertaining episode during a family supper or the common memory of a neighbor about a local area occasion, the significance of these unremarkable collaborations becomes obvious in the making of an aggregate memory that ties people and networks across time.

The purposeful development of positive ordinary connections adds to a culture of graciousness and sympathy. Thoughtful gestures, whether communicated through a grin, an expression of consolation, or a little token of help, have a gradually expanding influence that reaches out past the quick trade. In people group where positive regular cooperations are esteemed and focused on, a culture of generosity arises. This culture, thus, turns into a strong power for making a more empathetic culture, where people effectively look for potential chances to elevate and uphold each other in the embroidery of day to day existence.

Commonplace cooperations cultivate a feeling of social obligation and municipal commitment. With regards to networks and neighborhoods, ordinary associations add to the aggregate awareness of certain expectations for the prosperity of the entirety. Whether it's taking part in area watch programs, sorting out local area occasions, or teaming up on shared drives, the unremarkable trades structure the basis for a culture of dynamic citizenship. This feeling of obligation stretches out past individual families, making a common obligation to the improvement of the local area.

Regular cooperations become a vehicle for the transmission of social qualities and standards. Inside families, networks, and social orders, the passing down of social customs, values, and standards frequently happens over day to day existence. The manner in which families welcome one another, the customs related with everyday dinners, and the recognition of social works on during routine exercises add to the transmission of social personality. Along these lines, unremarkable communications become transporters of social legacy, guaranteeing its congruity and variation across ages.

Ordinary associations offer open doors for individual reflection and self-disclosure. In the normal trades with others, people experience impressions of themselves through the eyes of everyone around them. Ordinary cooperations give reflects that can uncover parts of one's character, correspondence style, and effect on others. This input circle turns into a wellspring of mindfulness, provoking people to consider their way of behaving, values, and the manner in which they add to the social elements of their nearby circles.

The corresponding idea of ordinary connections encourages a feeling of correspondence and shared help. The compromise innate in everyday trades makes a feeling of reliance among people. Whether it's assisting a neighbor with an undertaking, offering a listening ear to a companion, or teaming up on shared projects, the correspondence implanted in regular communications frames the bedrock of common encouraging groups of people. This feeling of shared dependence upgrades the strength of people and networks, making a security net woven through the texture of daily existence.

Everyday connections become a mirror mirroring the condition of cultural qualities and needs. Cultural standards, assumptions, and values are communicated through stupendous announcements as well as implanted in the details of day to day existence. The manner in which people cooperate, the ways of behaving that are supported or deterred in regular trades, and the needs that manifest in routine exercises all in all illustrate cultural qualities. By examining the examples of regular communications, one can recognize the common ethos of a general public and its goals for aggregate prosperity.

The interconnectedness of regular cooperations adds to the versatility of informal communities. In the midst of emergency or disturbance, the strength of social bonds turns into a basic calculate exploring difficulties. The consistency of ordinary connections, whether as standard registrations with companions, shared exercises inside networks, or familial encouraging groups of people, adds to the versatility of social designs. These organizations, sustained through ordinary trades, act as mainstays of help during troublesome times, accentuating the significant significance of these apparently commonplace minutes in the midst of hardship.

The assessment of the significance of commonplace, regular cooperations uncovers an embroidery woven with strings of the capacity to understand individuals on a profound level, shared stories, social coherence, and cultural qualities. These collaborations, frequently excused as normal, arise as the essential components that shape the nature of our lives, connections, and the cultural texture. As we explore the intricacies of human association, it becomes obvious that the meaning of ordinary cooperations lies in their straightforwardness as well as in their ability to impact individual prosperity, cultural elements, and the actual quintessence of being essential for a common human encounter.

2.2 Anecdotes highlighting how small, shared experiences build strong bonds.

In the mosaic of human connections, it is the apparently unimportant minutes, the murmurs of day to day existence, that make the orchestra out of association. These accounts unfurl as vignettes, representing how little, shared encounters become the mortar that ties the blocks major areas of strength for of between people, families, and networks.

In a clamoring metropolitan area, the everyday custom of a morning wave between two neighbors turned into a quiet settlement of fellowship. No words were traded, only a basic affirmation across the wall as one tasted espresso on the yard and the other watered the plants. Over the long haul, this implicit hello developed into a mutual perspective — the affirmation that, in the midst of the buzzing about, a snapshot of association could be tracked down in a basic wave. At the point when one neighbor became sick, it was the other who, without a second thought, stepped in to assist with tasks and deal truly necessary help. The bond produced through those day to day waves changed into a life saver during a difficult time, representing the extraordinary force of little, shared signals.

In the core of an affectionate family, the daily everyday practice of social occasion around the supper table turned into a valued custom. It wasn't just about the food; it was a custom of fellowship, a space for giggling, discusses, and the sharing of everyday tales. In the beat of passing dishes, pouring beverages, and clunking utensils, the family tracked down a safe-haven of association. As kids developed, this daily fellowship turned into the compass directing them through the difficulties of youthfulness. The common experience of fellowshipping together turned into the foundation of familial bonds, a demonstration of the getting through strength of little, steady ceremonies in building an underpinning of adoration and backing.

Inside the walls of a work environment, a common short breather among partners diverted into a day to day relief from the requests of the gig. The espresso machine turned into the background for a microcosm of connections, where the burdens of the working environment were quickly saved. In the relaxed chitchat over espresso, partners figured out something worth agreeing on, found shared interests, and, in particular, constructed an organization of trust. At the point when a venture confronted unanticipated difficulties, it was this kinship framed during those short quick rests that permitted the group to endure the hardship together. The unpretentious espresso machine turned into an impetus for cooperation and fortitude, epitomizing how shared snapshots of reprieve can invigorate proficient connections.

With regards to a local area garden, the demonstration of tending to shared plots turned into a representation for the interconnectedness of neighbors. As people weeded, planted, and supported their individual patches of green, a feeling of aggregate liability bloomed.

It wasn't just about private yields; it was tied in with adding to the excellence of the whole nursery. The common experience of cajoling life from the dirt turned into a common excursion, one where tips were traded, harvests were commended, and the back and forth movement of seasons reflected the rhythms of mutual residing. At the point when an especially cruel winter undermined the nursery, it was the aggregate exertion of neighbors covering and safeguarding the delicate shoots that displayed the strength brought into the world from shared liabilities.

On a school grounds, a review bunch shaped out of a common battle with a difficult course. What started as a down to earth collusion for scholarly help immediately changed into a very close friend network. Late-night concentrate on meetings transformed into open doors for shared giggling, common consolation, and, at times, the festival of little triumphs like at last embracing a complicated idea. As graduation drew nearer, it was this review bunch that remained as a demonstration of the persevering through force of shared difficulties. The bonds shaped during late-night pack meetings turned into the framework for persevering through companionships that reached out a long ways past the study hall.

Inside the walls of a permanent spot for the older, a week after week game night turned into a wellspring of euphoria and association for the occupants. The straightforward demonstration of playing a card game or table games changed the collective space into a safe house of shared giggling and cordial contest. As occupants participated in these games, companionships bloomed, and a feeling of local area prospered. At the point when one occupant confronted wellbeing challenges, it was the help and fellowship developed during those game evenings that turned into a wellspring of solace and friendship. The common encounters around the game table exemplified how even in the dusk long stretches of life, the bonds framed through little, shared exercises stay versatile.

With regards to a worker bunch, the common mission of having a constructive outcome on the local area turned into the paste that bound different people together. The errands they embraced — whether tidying up a nearby park, putting together occasions, or helping those out of luck — were the strings that wove an embroidery of mutual perspective. The common encounters of loaning some assistance and seeing the unmistakable effect on their local area made a feeling of satisfaction that rose above individual contrasts. At the point when outer difficulties tried the determination of the gathering, it was the common obligation to their main goal that assembled them in beating difficulty, featuring the extraordinary force of shared attempts.

Inside the limits of an emergency clinic lounge area, the common encounters of families confronting comparative difficulties fashioned associations that rose above the limits of sickness. As families explored the vulnerabilities of clinical medicines, the lounge area turned into a space for shared comfort and understanding. The trading of compassionate looks, the gestures of affirmation, and the implicit help shaped an undetectable organization of shared encounters.

At the point when one family got positive news, it was the commendation and shared euphoria from others in the lounge area that transformed a singular victory into a collective festival. The common flexibility and shared help turned into a demonstration of the strength that rises out of confronting misfortune together.

In a multicultural area, the demonstration of sharing customary dishes during bubbly seasons turned into a festival of variety and solidarity. Families opened their kitchens, sharing the fragrances and kinds of their social legacy. The collective tables turned into a mixture of culinary encounters, where neighbors tasted different foods as well as found out about the tales, customs, and chronicles behind each dish. The demonstration of sharing food turned into a strong extension, encouraging comprehension and appreciation for the rich embroidery of societies inside the area. At the point when difficulties emerged, it was the solidarity fashioned through these culinary trades that permitted the local area to explore social contrasts with deference and sympathy.

Inside the circle of a kinship, the common encounters of exploring life's achievements made a bond that endured everyday hardship. From commending accomplishments to supporting each other during difficulties, the common excursion of development and self-revelation turned into the underpinning of a persevering through fellowship. At the point when one companion confronted a junction, it was the common history of wins and hardships that gave the compass to direction and backing. The bond framed through long periods of shared encounters turned into a life saver, outlining the versatility and profundity of associations supported through the embroidery of daily existence.

In the fabulous woven artwork of human association, these tales enlighten the extraordinary force of little, shared encounters. They uncover that it isn't the size of occasions yet the consistency of shared minutes that fashions enduring bonds. Whether through routine good tidings, familial customs, work environment collaborations, or local area attempts, the quintessence of association lies in the normal, the commonplace, and the regular. These tales act as a demonstration of the persevering through truth that it is inside the common strings of chuckling, backing, and understanding that the most grounded bonds are woven — an embroidery rich with the shades of shared encounters.

In the material of kinship, the unconstrained excursions turned into the strings winding around a permanent example of shared experiences. What started as un-rehearsed choices to get away from the dreariness of day to day existence developed into a practice of investigation and revelation. The common snapshots of exploring new streets, belting out most loved tunes, and halting at side of the road cafes made a mosaic of recollections that characterized the quintessence of their kinship. At the point when life introduced difficulties, it was the reverberations of chuckling from those travels that filled in as a sign of the flexibility and bliss implanted in their common process.

Inside the setting of a book club, the common investigation of scholarly universes turned into the impetus for significant conversations and profound associations. The demonstration of perusing a similar book and meeting up to take apart its subtleties changed into a custom of scholarly fellowship. The common encounters of deciphering characters, taking apart unexpected developments, and investigating different stories encouraged a climate where fellowships rose above the limits of the book club gatherings. At the point when one part confronted an individual battle, it was the compassion and backing woven through those scholarly conversations that transformed the book club into a safe-haven of common perspective.

In the hug of nature, the common dawn customs among a gathering of companions turned into a wellspring of motivation and otherworldly association. Whether on a mountain or by the shore, the demonstration of seeing the dawn together turned into a consecrated snapshot of recharging and shared examination. The common encoun-ters of hello the day break, with its tones of gold and pink, turned into an indication of the transient yet everlasting nature of life. At the point when one companion defied a time of thoughtfulness, it was the common recollections of those dawn social events that offered comfort and a feeling of interconnectedness with an option that could be bigger than themselves.

Inside the elements of a nurturing support bunch, the common difficulties and wins of bringing up kids turned into the establishment for persevering through kin-ships. From restless evenings to initial steps, the assemble explored the rollercoaster of life as a parent together. The common encounters of trading tips, consoling each other during difficult stretches, and praising the little triumphs shaped a bond that reached out past playdates and nurturing exhortation. At the point when one parent confronted a huge life progress, it was the common excursion of being a parent that gave an organization of understanding and backing, underlining the job of shared encounters in manufacturing enduring associations.

With regards to a local area ensemble, the common energy for music turned into the amicable string that bound people with different foundations. The demonstration of meeting up to make music rose above contrasts, encouraging a feeling of solidarity and joint effort. The common encounters of practices, exhibitions, and the aggregate quest for creative articulation turned into the core of their association. At the point when the local area confronted outer difficulties, it was the common tunes and the public soul developed through the ensemble that turned into a wellspring of flexibility, featuring the extraordinary force of shared inventive undertakings.

These extra tales further highlight the mind boggling exchange of shared encounters in serious areas of strength for building. From unconstrained excursions and artistic conversations to dawn customs, nurturing difficulties, and the cooperative making of music, these accounts enlighten the different manners by which shared minutes add to the embroidered artwork of human association.

Every tale uncovers that it is inside the common strings of chuckling, understanding, and aggregate undertakings that the texture of enduring bonds is unpredictably woven — a demonstration of the getting through force of shared encounters in molding the mosaic of human connections.

2.3 Reflection on the significance of seemingly insignificant moments.

In the excellent woven artwork of life, it is much of the time the strings of apparently irrelevant minutes that weave the most significant and persevering through designs. These minutes, brief and sensitive, hold inside them the pith of our reality, molding our connections, viewpoints, and the actual texture of our common humankind. In this intelligent investigation, we dig into the meaning of these apparently unnoticeable minutes, disentangling the profundity they bring to the human experience.

The Inconspicuous Dance of Everyday Schedules:

In the tranquil rhythm of everyday schedules lies an unobtrusive dance that characterizes the mood of our lives. The wake-up routine of tasting some espresso, the recognizable course we take to work, the common looks with a neighbor during a night walk — these are the little movements that make the ambient sound out of our reality. While effortlessly excused as commonplace, these schedules ground us one might say of commonality and congruity. It is in the reiteration of these apparently unimportant demonstrations that we track down dependability and a consoling steadiness in the midst of the consistently changing scene of life.

The Language of Microexpressions:

Inside the theater of human connections, it is the microexpressions — the short flash of a grin, the inconspicuous wrinkle of a temple — that say a lot. These temporary snapshots of non-verbal correspondence structure a perplexing language that rises above words. Amidst a packed room, the traded looks between companions convey a mutual perspective; in a snapshot of challenge, the consoling gesture from a partner discusses fortitude. These microexpressions are the quiet comments to the account of our connections, adding layers of subtlety and profundity to the narratives we share with others.

Murmurs of Nature:

In the hug of nature, apparently irrelevant minutes unfurl as murmurs that reverberation through our spirits. The delicate stir of leaves in a separated timberland, the fragile dance of daylight on a dew-kissed morning, or the short lived look at a bird in flight — all are parts of the bigger ensemble of the regular world. These minutes, not entirely obvious in that frame of mind of current life, act as tokens of our interconnectedness with the earth. They welcome us to stop, inhale, and adjust ourselves to the inconspicuous rhythms of the regular world, offering comfort and a feeling of having a place.

The Orchestra of Little Signals:

Inside the domain of connections, the orchestra of little motions makes the most essential songs. A transcribed note got into a lunchbox, an unconstrained embrace from a companion, or the common chuckling over some tea — these motions, apparently unimportant, are the brushstrokes that paint the profound material of our associations. In the back and forth movement of day to day associations, it is the combined impact of these little, ardent minutes that forms scaffolds of trust, develops closeness, and reinforces the bonds that attach us to each other.

The Dance of Dusks and Dawns:

The divine artful dance of nightfalls and dawns fills in as an immortal material on which the excellence of presence is painted once again every day. Whether saw in isolation or imparted to friends and family, these heavenly changes offer snapshots of reflection and wonder. In the blurring tints of nightfall or the delicate shine of day break, there is a beautiful sign of the transient idea of life. Apparently unimportant in their normal event, dusks and dawns become customs of association, welcoming us to wonder about the loftiness of the universe and track down comfort in the coherence of heavenly rhythms.

Brief looks at Shared Mankind:

In the mosaic of mankind, the brief looks at shared encounters break down the deception of partition. The common grin with an outsider on a packed train, the gesture of affirmation from somebody confronting comparable difficulties, or the deep breath of help in a snapshot of collective satisfaction — these are the fastens that patch the embroidery of our common presence. In these apparently unimportant minutes, the limits among self and other haze, uncovering the interconnectedness that characterizes the human experience.

In the Quietness Between Words:

While words convey unequivocal implications, frequently the quietness between them conveys the heaviness of implicit bits of insight. In discussions with friends and family, the pregnant respite before an admission, or the calm snapshots of reflection partook in helpful quietness, the implicit language resounds profoundly. Apparently unimportant, the stops and hushes consider the implied to wait in the air, cultivating a significant comprehension that rises above verbal articulation.

Temporary Looks at Self-Disclosure:

Inside the peaceful corners of contemplation, apparently inconsequential minutes become mirrors reflecting parts of our own being. A passing thought, a snapshot of acknowledgment in the mirror, or the unobtrusive acknowledgment during a single walk — these are the parts of self-disclosure. Chasing after excellent accounts, it is these momentary looks into our own spirits that guide us toward grasping, acknowledgment, and the constant excursion of becoming.

The Range of Normal Excellence:

In the midst of the clatter for remarkable encounters, the range of normal excellence colors the material of our lives. The petals of a side of the road bloom, the play of shadows on a peaceful evening, or the impression of city lights on downpour kissed roads — these are the strokes that make the magnum opus out of our regular presence. Apparently immaterial, these minutes welcome us to track down magnificence in the conventional, to see the value in the extravagance woven into the texture of our day to day routines.

The Dance of Good fortune:

In the domain of good fortune, apparently irrelevant minutes disclose the enchantment of the unforeseen. An opportunity experience with a close buddy in a clamoring city, the disclosure of an unlikely treasure during an unconstrained excursion, or the impromptu diversion that prompts a stunning perspective — these are the moves of good fortune. Apparently immaterial in their unusualness, these minutes implant our lives with immediacy, shock, and the superb acknowledgment that sorcery frequently dwells in the impromptu.

The Reverberations of Life as a youngster Blamelessness:

In the wistfulness of lifelong recollections, apparently irrelevant minutes reverberation with the guiltlessness of youth. The chuckling shared during jungle gym games, the flavor of a most loved treat, or the delight of finding the world once more — these are the reverberations that resound across the years. Apparently unimportant in their promptness, these minutes become valuable sections of our own accounts, helping us to remember the immaculateness and marvel that once characterized our point of view.

The Scent of Basic Delights:

Inside the domain of basic delights, apparently unimportant minutes unfurl as scents that wait in our recollections. The fragrance of downpour doused earth, the smell of a home-prepared dinner, or the scent of a friend or family member's hug — these olfactory depictions become bookmarks in the parts of our lives. Apparently ordinary, these minutes convey the heaviness of sentimentality, summoning a feeling of solace and association with the past.

Appearance in Still Waters:

In snapshots of quietness, apparently unimportant reflections on still waters uncover significant bits of insight. Whether looking into a serene lake, noticing the reflected pictures in a lake, or considering the undulating surface of a waterway, these minutes become illustrations for thoughtfulness. Apparently peaceful, these reflections welcome us to dive into the profundities of our own considerations, feelings, and the supplies of intelligence that exist in.

The Group of stars of Shared Giggling:

In the domain of shared euphoria, apparently immaterial minutes unwind as heavenly bodies of shared chuckling.

Whether ejecting during an easygoing discussion, reverberating through a family supper, or resounding in the organization of companions, these explosions of merriment become the stars that enlighten the night sky of our aggregate encounters. Apparently transient, shared giggling turns into a heavenly body that diagrams the course of our common satisfaction.

The Verse of Implicit Bonds:

Inside the verse of connections, apparently immaterial minutes are the implicit stanzas that make the story out of association. A delicate touch during a snapshot of weakness, the common look that imparts volumes, or the quiet presence during seasons of isolation — these are the stanzas that convey the profundity of close to home securities. Apparently basic, these minutes become the stanzas that portray the perplexing story of shared lives.

Forms of Self-improvement:

In the scene of self-awareness, apparently unimportant minutes cut the forms of our developing selves. The tranquil choice to embrace change, the little triumphs notwithstanding affliction, or the unpretentious advances taken toward personal development — these minutes become the structure blocks of our own accounts. Apparently mediocre, these minutes uncover the versatility, fortitude, and tirelessness that shape the direction of our singular processes.

The Embroidery of Social Association:

Inside the embroidery of social legacy, apparently inconsequential minutes become strings that weave the lavishness of shared customs. The ceremonies went down through ages, the natural tunes of society melodies, or the readiness of respected recipes — these are the social markers that anchor networks one might say of personality. Apparently standard, these minutes become the strings that support the progression of social inheritances.

The Rhythm of Shared Quiet:

In the rhythm of shared quiet, apparently immaterial minutes unfurl as reflective stops that extend associations. Whether sitting next to each other in calm friendship or partaking in an aggregate snapshot of reflection, shared quiet turns into its very own language. Apparently absent any and all activity, these minutes reverberate with a significant comprehension that rises above words, cultivating a feeling of solidarity and shared thought.

The Ethereal Dance of Concealed Consideration:

Inside the domain of generosity, apparently unimportant minutes unfurl as the ethereal dance of inconspicuous signals. An entryway held open for a more unusual, a cautious demonstration of good cause, or the calm help reached out without show — these are the strings of thoughtfulness that wind through the texture of our networks.

Apparently mediocre, these minutes swell outward, making an embroidery of generosity that elevates the aggregate soul.

The Hug of Unrestricted Love:

In the safe-haven of adoration, apparently immaterial minutes unfurl as the hug of unqualified warmth. The implicit consolation in a parent's look, the tranquil pardoning traded between accomplices, or the unlimited euphoria according to a pet — these are the declarations of adoration that rise above the requirement for terrific signals. Apparently normal, these minutes become the mainstays of persevering through connections, typifying the significant truth that adoration lives in the effortlessness of shared minutes.

Agreement in Shared Points of view:

In the agreeable trade of points of view, apparently immaterial minutes become the notes that make the orchestra out of aggregate comprehension. The eagerness to tune in during a conflict, the common affirmation of different perspectives, or the cooperative work to connect contrasts — these minutes become the harmonies that blend connections. Apparently unpretentious, these minutes add to the making of a common story that praises variety and encourages solidarity.

The Dance of Instinctive Inventiveness:

Inside the dance of inventive articulation, apparently irrelevant minutes unfurl as unconstrained explosions of motivation. The extemporaneous doodle during a gathering, the unusual creation brought into the world from a snapshot of fatigue, or the unstructured play with imaginative mediums — these are the statements of natural inventiveness. Apparently indiscriminate, these minutes become the flashes that touch off the flames of advancement and self-articulation.

A Tribute to Apparently Inconsequential Minutes:

In the excellent coordination of life, these reflections act as a tribute to the apparently irrelevant minutes that make the story out of our reality. It is a festival of the murmurs, looks, and signals that frequently slip through the cracks in the embroidery of our regular routines. It is an affirmation of the significant effect implanted in the texture of the conventional, the ordinary, and the apparently unimportant. These minutes, similar to parts of stardust, shimmer in the immense breadth of our recollections, advising us that importance frequently stays in the tranquil spaces between the vainglorious achievements.

The Gradually expanding influence of Apparently Unimportant Minutes:

The meaning of apparently immaterial minutes resonates a long ways past their nearby effect. Like waves on the outer layer of a lake, these minutes expand their impact, forming the shapes of our daily routines and the existences of people around us. A little thoughtful gesture, a common grin, or a snapshot of understanding makes an expanding influence that fountains through the interconnected trap of human connections. In the embroidery of local area and society, these apparently paltry minutes add to the making of a culture of sympathy, empathy, and aggregate prosperity.

Consider a situation where an outsider stretches out some assistance to somebody out of luck — a go about as basic as holding the entryway open for somebody battling with sacks. At that time, the beneficiary of this little motion not just encounters a functional mitigation of a weight yet additionally gets a close to home lift. The affirmation that somebody wants to think about it, even in a brief experience, turns into a wellspring of energy. This profound elevate, but short, impacts the beneficiary's resulting connections, possibly rousing them to pay the consideration forward. The far reaching influence starts, and the underlying apparently irrelevant second turns into an impetus for a chain of positive cooperations, molding the social texture in unobtrusive however significant ways.

The Development of Memory:

Apparently inconsequential minutes, as they aggregate over the long run, add to the mosaic of our recollections. While great occasions might shape the tops in the scene of memories, the bunch of apparently little minutes fill the valleys, giving profundity and surface to our own stories. A common snicker during an easygoing discussion, the fragrance of a natural scent, or the glow of a soothing touch — these sections of daily existence become the structure blocks of treasured recollections.

In the display of shared encounters, apparently irrelevant minutes become the close to home anchors that tie us to explicit periods in our lives. A specific tune playing on the radio during an everyday drive or the flavor of a youth treat can move us back in time, evoking a surge of recollections related with those apparently paltry minutes. Along these lines, these minutes become the imperceptible ink engraved upon the pages of our own accounts, making a permanent imprint that shapes our healthy identity and our association with the past.

The Powerful Woven artwork of Self-improvement:

Apparently unimportant minutes assume a crucial part in the powerful embroidery of self-awareness. It is in many cases the little, steady endeavors, the gradual advances taken toward personal growth, that lead to groundbreaking change over the long haul. Consider the individual who chooses to embrace a better way of life. While significant achievements, for example, weight reduction objectives or wellness accomplishments might snatch consideration, it is the apparently irrelevant everyday decisions — deciding on a piece of natural product rather than a sweet tidbit, using the stairwell rather than the lift — that by and large add to a better and more healthy lifestyle.

These little snapshots of decision and discipline become the establishment whereupon bigger changes are constructed. After some time, the combined impact of apparently irrelevant choices becomes obvious, in actual prosperity as well as in the improvement of flexibility, discipline, and a positive mentality. The excursion of self-awareness is stamped by huge achievements as well as by the reliable string of little, deliberate decisions made in the peaceful corners of day to day existence.

The Dance of Shared Weakness:

In the domain of connections, apparently irrelevant minutes become the dance of shared weakness. It is much of the time in the unguarded minutes, the unscripted trades, that the genuine embodiment of association is uncovered. A common look during a snapshot of vulnerability, a veritable articulation of concern, or the confirmation of an individual battle — these apparently subtle minutes become the strings that weave the embroidery of closeness.

Think about the companions who, in a snapshot of weakness, share their feelings of dread, dreams, and uncertainties. While these minutes may not be fantastic announcements of adoration or significant life disclosures, they structure the premise of trust and profound closeness. The readiness to be open, even in apparently little ways, makes a space for credibility and certified association. In the dance of shared weakness, people track down comfort, understanding, and a feeling of being really seen and acknowledged.

The String of Shared Customs:

Apparently immaterial minutes gain importance when woven into shared ceremonies and schedules. Whether it's the daily family supper, the Sunday morning espresso date with a companion, or the yearly custom of occasion social events, these minutes become the strings that tight spot people into a feeling of aggregate character and having a place. The redundancy of apparently unremarkable exercises takes on a groundbreaking quality when instilled with shared significance and expectation.

With regards to a family, for instance, the sleep time routine of perusing a story to a youngster might appear to be a little, ordinary event. Nonetheless, this apparently unimportant second turns into a string that reinforces the parent-kid bond. After some time, the consistency of such customs adds to the kid's feeling of safety, encouraging profound association and an underpinning of trust. Shared ceremonies, regardless of whether at first humble, gather into a repository of shared encounters that characterize the remarkable personality and union of a gathering.

The Transient Excellence of Ordinary Feel:

In the domain of style, apparently irrelevant minutes unfurl as vaporous excellence that encompasses us in the embroidered artwork of regular daily existence. The play of daylight through leaves, the impression of city lights on downpour splashed roads, or the many-sided subtleties of normal items — all add to a visual ensemble that frequently slips by everyone's notice in the surge of present day life. However, these snapshots of visual verse have the ability to lift our spirits, rouse inventiveness, and cultivate a feeling of marvel.

Think about the straightforward demonstration of going for a careful stroll through a recognizable area. In this apparently immaterial second, the onlooker might find the unpretentious subtleties that change the conventional into the uncommon — the surface of a block facade, the example of fallen leaves, or the exchange of shadows and light.

The enthusiasm for these regular style turns into an act of care, welcoming people to track down magnificence in the apparently commonplace and implanting their day to day routines with a feeling of veneration for the standard.

The Embodiment of Careful Presence:

At the core of the meaning of apparently immaterial minutes lies the quintessence of careful presence. In a world frequently portrayed by steady development and clamor, these minutes act as solicitations to be completely present in the unfurling embroidery of our lives. The demonstration of relishing some tea, experiencing the glow of daylight on the skin, or essentially being completely mindful during a discussion — all are articulations of careful presence.

With regards to connections, careful presence turns into a strong gift. At the point when people effectively participate in apparently immaterial minutes with complete focus and credibility, they sign to others that they are esteemed and seen. The demonstration of listening mindfully, sharing a veritable grin, or offering a soothing touch — all become indications of careful presence that rise above the impediments of existence.

The Insight of Apparently Irrelevant Minutes:

In the last examination, the meaning of apparently irrelevant minutes uncovers itself as a storehouse of shrewdness — a complicated guide that guides us through the scenes of our lives. These minutes show us the specialty of appreciation, empowering us to track down happiness in the conventional and excellence in the everyday. They give the illustration of association, helping us that the strings to remember shared encounters, regardless of how little, weave the texture of significant connections and collective bonds.

Apparently immaterial minutes enlighten the way of care, asking us to be completely present in the unfurling excursion of our lives. They highlight the force of consistency and deliberateness, uncovering that extraordinary change frequently starts in the tranquil corners of day to day existence. In the amazing account of self-improvement, connections, and the human experience, these minutes act as both the establishment and the embellishments that advance the tale of our reality.

As we explore the mind boggling woven artwork of life, may we develop a familiarity with the importance implanted in these apparently subtle minutes. In the orchestra of presence, may we adjust our faculties to the songs of shared chuckling, the rhythms of everyday schedules, and the harmonies of shared weakness. For it is in the careful hug of these apparently immaterial minutes that we find the significant excellence woven into the actual texture of our lives — a marvel that rises above the vaporous idea of time and leaves a persevering through engrave on the material of our common humankind.

Chapter 3

"Roles and Responsibilities"

In the perplexing dance of life, people take on different jobs and obligations, wearing various caps as they explore the multi-layered scenes of individual, proficient, and cultural circles. This broad investigation looks to disentangle the woven artwork of jobs and obligations, inspecting how these unique components shape the forms of character, connections, and the aggregate structure holding the system together.

Individual Jobs:

At the center of individual character lie individual jobs, the jobs one expects inside the setting of oneself. These jobs include the horde features of individual life, from being a child or little girl to taking on the obligations of a companion, accomplice, or parent. The job of a kin, for example, may involve offering help, sharing encounters, and encouraging familial bonds. As a companion, the obligations might incorporate sympathy, friendship, and shared support.

The job of an accomplice includes shared liabilities inside a heartfelt connection, like correspondence, split the difference, and daily reassurance. Being a parent delivers a special arrangement of jobs, requesting supporting, direction, and the arrangement of a protected climate for the development of kids. These individual jobs interlace to frame the perplexing mosaic of individual personality, affecting activities, choices, and the general identity.

Proficient Jobs:

In the domain of expert life, people step into particular jobs characterized by their occupations, positions, and obligations inside authoritative designs. The job of a pioneer, for example, includes the direction and bearing of a group or a whole association. Pioneers shoulder the obligation of independent direction, motivating others, and making a dream that pushes the aggregate exertion forward.

Representatives inside an association assume parts going from experts to colleagues, each contributing remarkable abilities and mastery. The obligations related with proficient jobs stretch out past individual errands, enveloping coordinated effort, adherence to moral norms, and the quest for authoritative objectives. The powerful interaction of these jobs frames the foundation of the expert world, molding the way of life, efficiency, and progress of ventures.

Social Jobs:

Past private and expert areas, people occupy jobs inside the more extensive cultural setting. Citizenship, for example, is a central social job that involves liabilities, for example, submitting to regulations, taking part in urban exercises, and adding to the prosperity of the local area. Backing jobs include bringing issues to light about friendly issues and supporting positive change.

The job of a coach or instructor is basic to the transmission of information and values across ages. In these social jobs, people become specialists of impact, adding to the aggregate development and progress of society. Obligations stretch out to advancing inclusivity, equity, and reasonable works on, cultivating a feeling of shared responsibility for the government assistance of the more extensive local area.

Orientation Jobs:

In numerous social orders, orientation jobs have generally endorsed explicit assumptions and responsibilities regarding people in light of their orientation. These jobs frequently impact familial elements, with assumptions about providing care, family obligations, and vocation pursuits. Be that as it may, advancing cultural standards and developments upholding for orientation uniformity have tested and reshaped these customary jobs.

Ladies, generally appointed jobs revolved around homegrown obligations, have progressively taken on different jobs in the expert field, the scholarly world, and public life. Men, once bound to explicit assumptions connected with strength and supplier jobs, are currently exploring advancing meanings of manliness that embrace the capacity to understand anyone on a deeper level, providing care, and cooperative methodologies. The continuous exchange around orientation jobs mirrors a more extensive cultural shift towards perceiving individual capacities and destroying prohibitive generalizations.

Social and Ethnic Jobs:

Social and ethnic characters contribute extra layers to the jobs people expect. These jobs envelop practices, customs, and obligations attached to one's social legacy. In multicultural social orders, people frequently explore the sensitive equilibrium of saving their social character while partaking in the more extensive social woven artwork.

Social jobs include the transmission of customs, ceremonies, and values to resulting ages. People might take on liabilities inside their social networks, partaking in festivals, safeguarding language, and encouraging a feeling of having a place. In different social orders, the trading of social jobs adds to a rich and dynamic social scene, testing generalizations and encouraging common comprehension.

Strict and Profound Jobs:

Strict and profound convictions give a structure to the jobs people play inside their networks and the more extensive world. Jobs inside strict settings can go from the obligations of a believer to those of strict pioneers or teachers. People might be called upon to satisfy obligations connected with local area administration, altruistic exercises, or the advancement of virtues.

The job of an otherworldly aide or tutor includes offering help, direction, and working with the profound development of others. The obligations related with strict and otherworldly jobs frequently stretch out past individual prosperity to include local area union, moral lead, and the quest for a higher reason.

Innovative Jobs:

In the computerized age, mechanical headways have acquainted new aspects with the jobs people play. The job of a computerized resident, for example, includes liabilities connected with online behavior, advanced education, and the moral utilization of innovation. As clients of web-based entertainment stages, people may likewise take on jobs as happy makers, powerhouses, or supporters inside virtual networks.

Experts in the innovation area expect jobs that drive development, address moral contemplations, and add to the improvement of a worldwide computerized society. The obligations related with mechanical jobs incorporate defending protection, tending to network safety concerns, and guaranteeing evenhanded admittance to innovative assets.

Ecological Jobs:

Notwithstanding worldwide natural difficulties, people are progressively taking on jobs with obligations toward the planet. The job of an ecological steward includes manageable practices, preservation endeavors, and promotion for approaches that address environmental change. Obligations stretch out to decreasing biological impressions, advancing biodiversity, and bringing issues to light about ecological issues.

In proficient settings, people might take on jobs zeroed in on natural manageability, consolidating eco-accommodating practices into business tasks. The aggregate reception of ecological jobs is crucial for the prosperity of the planet and the conservation of normal assets for people in the future.

Jobs in Struggle and Goal:

In settings set apart by struggle, people might end up in jobs that request exchange, intercession, and compromise. The job of a middle person includes working with correspondence between clashing gatherings to arrive at a commonly pleasant goal. Obligations incorporate keeping up with fair-mindedness, cultivating understanding, and directing the interaction toward a tranquil result.

People engaged with compromise jobs might work inside networks, associations, or global settings. These jobs have a significant impact in moderating strains, advancing discourse, and adding to the foundation of manageable harmony.

Jobs in Providing care and Medical services:

The jobs related with providing care and medical services include significant obligations connected with the prosperity and wellbeing of people. The job of a medical services proficient includes undertakings going from conclusion and therapy to preventive consideration and patient instruction. These jobs require skill, sympathy, and a pledge to moral norms.

In providing care jobs inside families, people might take on obligations connected with the consideration of youngsters, older relatives, or people with exceptional necessities. The obligations related with these jobs reach out past actual consideration to consistent encouragement, backing for medical services access, and exploring complex medical care frameworks.

Instructive Jobs:

Jobs inside instructive settings range a range, from instructors and heads to understudies and guardians. The job of an instructor includes the transmission of information, the encouraging of decisive reasoning abilities, and the development of a positive learning climate. Instructive overseers might expect jobs connected with strategy improvement, educational program plan, and the general administration of instructive foundations.

Understudies, thus, take on jobs as students, teammates, and supporters of the instructive local area. Guardians might participate in jobs connected with supporting their kids' schooling, taking part in parent-educator affiliations, and pushing for instructive assets.

Monetary Jobs:

In monetary frameworks, people assume parts as shoppers, makers, and supporters of financial exercises.

The job of a buyer includes going with decisions about the distribution of assets through buying choices. Makers, whether in business or horticulture, accept jobs connected with the creation and dissemination of labor and products.

People participated in monetary jobs add to the working of business sectors, the development of ventures, and the by and large financial wellbeing of networks and countries. Obligations incorporate moral strategic approaches, monetary education, and the quest for financial exercises that advance maintainability.

Jobs in Administration and Authority:

Inside the setting of administration and initiative, people might expect jobs that impact navigation, strategy improvement, and the course of networks or countries. Political pioneers, chose authorities, and policymakers take on jobs with huge obligations connected with the government assistance of their constituents. These obligations incorporate the plan of regulations, the designation of assets, and the advancement of equity and value.

Residents inside fair social orders accept jobs as electors, activists, and members in urban life. The obligations related with these jobs include remaining informed about policy centered issues, taking part in exchange, and adding to the vote based process.

Jobs in Expressions and Articulation:

In the domain of expressions and articulation, people take on jobs as makers, entertainers, and appreciators of imaginative undertakings. The job of a craftsman includes the statement of thoughts, feelings, and points of view through different mediums, from visual expressions and writing to music and performing expressions. Crowds, thusly, accept jobs as appreciators, pundits, and supporters of the social talk.

Imaginative jobs frequently convey liabilities connected with the investigation of cultural subjects, the difficult of standards, and the advancement of different points of view. The interchange of these jobs adds to the social wealth and innovative dynamic quality of social orders.

Jobs in Altruism and Social Activism:

Chasing after friendly effect and positive change, people frequently expect jobs inside the domains of altruism and social activism. The job of a donor includes contributing assets, monetary etc., to worthy missions that address social issues. Social activists take on jobs that include support, mindfulness raising, and endeavors to impact foundational change.

The obligations related with these jobs reach out to recognizing squeezing social issues, teaming up with associations, and activating assets to address difficulties. People took part in charity and social activism assume vital parts in driving cultural advancement and tending to imbalances.

Jobs in Sports and Diversion:

Inside the circle of sports and amusement, people accept jobs as competitors, mentors, and devotees. The job of a competitor includes thorough preparation, rivalry, and adherence to moral guidelines. Mentors assume parts in directing and coaching competitors, bestowing abilities, and cultivating a culture of cooperation.

Sports lovers add to the aggregate insight through their help, commitment, and support in sporting exercises. Obligations inside these jobs reach out to fair play, sportsmanship, and the advancement of actual prosperity.

Jobs in Advancement and Exploration:

Advancement and research jobs include people at the bleeding edge of propelling information, innovation, and logical comprehension. Researchers, specialists, and pioneers expect jobs connected with disclosure, trial and error, and the advancement of answers for complex difficulties. These jobs frequently convey responsibilities regarding moral direct, the spread of information, and the utilization of disclosures to improve society.

People participated in development and exploration add to the advancement of mankind, pushing the limits of what is known and driving progressions that shape what's to come.

Jobs in Correspondence and Media:

In the period of data, people assume parts in correspondence and media that impact public talk, shape accounts, and work with the trading of thoughts. Writers, editors, and media experts take on jobs with obligations connected with genuine revealing, moral reporting, and the spread of data. The job of a communicator stretches out to different stages, including online entertainment, where people add to public discussions and impact feelings.

The obligations related with correspondence jobs incorporate precision, straightforwardness, and the advancement of different voices. People taking part in these jobs add to the arrangement of general assessment and the forming of cultural accounts.

Jobs in Innovation and Man-made consciousness:

As innovation keeps on advancing, people wind up in jobs that cross with man-made reasoning, robotization, and computerized advancement. The job of a technologist includes the creation, improvement, and execution of innovative arrangements. In jobs connected with man-made reasoning, people wrestle with moral contemplations, the effect on business, and the dependable utilization of trend setting innovations.

3.1 Discussion on how responsibilities are distributed in a small family.

In the cozy setting of a little family, the dispersion of obligations is a fragile movement that shapes the everyday mood and long haul elements of the unit. Not at all like bigger family structures, where jobs might be more specific, the more modest family core frequently requires a more flexible way to deal with liabilities. In this conversation, we investigate how obligations are conveyed inside the setting of a little family, looking at the nuanced transaction of jobs and the elements that impact their portion.

Dynamic Nature of Little Family Designs:

Little families, ordinarily involving guardians and a predetermined number of kids, work inside a more contained and personal structure. The elements inside little families are portrayed by close communications, elevated profound associations, and a common feeling of obligation for the aggregate prosperity. Dissimilar to bigger families with broadened organizations of family members, the jobs in little families are many times more diverse, requiring every part to contribute across a range of liabilities.

The dissemination of obligations in a little family isn't static; rather, it develops because of different variables, including the age and formative phases of relatives, individual limits, and outside conditions. In the early long periods of life as a parent, for example, obligations might be prevalently based on childcare, with guardians taking on jobs as essential parental figures. As youngsters develop, the dispersion might move to incorporate instructive help, extracurricular inclusion, and shared navigation.

Parental Jobs and the Groundwork of Help:

Fundamental to the little family structure are the jobs of guardians, who frequently act as the essential modelers of the family's ethos and day to day working. Parental obligations incorporate a wide range, including yet not restricted to offering profound help, guaranteeing actual prosperity, bestowing values and schooling, and establishing a supporting climate. The division of these obligations frequently lines up with cultural standards but on the other hand is impacted by the one of a kind elements of the nuclear family.

Moms, generally connected with sustaining and providing care jobs, frequently take on liabilities connected with the close to home and actual prosperity of the family. From dealing with the family to offering profound help, moms assume a focal part in establishing a supporting climate. Fathers, then again, may generally take on obligations connected with monetary arrangement, discipline, and certain common-sense parts of family the board.

Nonetheless, perceiving the developing idea of parental jobs inside the setting of current little families is vital. As cultural standards shift towards more noteworthy orientation fairness, there is a developing pattern of divided liabilities among guardians. Fathers effectively take part in childcare, consistent reassurance, and family the executives, while moms might add to monetary choices and profession pursuits. This adaptability and flexibility in jobs add to a more adjusted and fair relational peculiarity.

Youngsters' Jobs and the Elements of Development:

The dispersion of obligations in a little family stretches out to the jobs that kids play inside the unit. While kids are beneficiaries of care and direction, they likewise add to the family's working in significant ways. The assignment of obligations to kids is in many cases formed by their age, formative stage, and the qualities imparted by the guardians.

In the early years, youngsters might be essentially beneficiaries of care, with guardians expecting jobs as suppliers and nurturers. As youngsters develop, their jobs extend to incorporate liabilities connected with their schooling, self-awareness, and commitments to family tasks. These obligations, frequently outlined as any open doors for learning and strengthening, assume a urgent part in molding kids' feeling of organization and self-viability.

Guardians, in little families, frequently include youngsters in dynamic cycles, empowering a feeling of obligation and responsibility. This might incorporate decisions connected with family exercises, monetary preparation, or even parts of day to day schedules. By effectively captivating youngsters in these cycles, guardians cultivate a cooperative and participatory family culture, supporting that obligations are shared and add to the aggregate prosperity.

Family Obligations and the Difficult exercise:

A critical component of obligation circulation in little families rotates around family the executives. The errands related with keeping a home, from cleaning and cooking to monetary administration, require a cooperative exertion among relatives. Not at all like bigger families where obligations might be more specific, the more modest nuclear family frequently requires a more adjusted and versatile methodology.

The conveyance of family obligations is affected by different variables, including work responsibilities, individual qualities, and inclinations. In certain families, there might be a more conventional division of work, with one parent taking on specific errands while the other spotlights on various perspectives. Nonetheless, in numerous cutting edge little families, there is a pattern towards a more evenhanded dispersion of family obligations, regardless of orientation jobs.

This impartial methodology frequently includes open correspondence and exchange between relatives.

It perceives that every part's significant investment are important and that a co-operative exertion upgrades the general nature of day to day life. The difficult exercise might include a mix of shared tasks, staggered liabilities, and a common obligation to keeping an amicable living climate.

Flexibility to Evolving Conditions:

One of the principal attributes of little family structures is their flexibility to evolving conditions. As relatives age, as outside variables, for example, vocation changes or medical problems become an integral factor, the dissemination of obligations might go through shifts. The capacity to adjust and rethink jobs becomes critical in keeping up with the prosperity and versatility of the nuclear family.

For instance, assuming a parent takes on another expert job that requests additional significant investment, there might be a brief reallocation of obligations inside the family. Essentially, in the event that a youngster enters a requesting scholarly stage or faces individual difficulties, the family might change jobs to offer the vital help and consolation. This flexibility mirrors the responsiveness of little families to the developing necessities and elements of every part.

The versatility likewise stretches out to the acknowledgment of individual qualities and interests. In a little family, there is many times more prominent familiarity with every part's remarkable gifts and inclinations. This mindfulness considers a more essential conveyance of obligations, adjusting errands to individual qualities and cultivating a feeling of satisfaction and achievement.

Correspondence as a Mainstay of Obligation Dissemination:

Fundamental to the compelling circulation of obligations in a little family is open and clear correspondence. The capacity of relatives to communicate their requirements, inclinations, and difficulties makes an establishment for cooperative direction. Normal family gatherings, conversations about objectives and needs, and a climate that energizes undivided attention all add to a solid correspondence system.

Correspondence turns out to be especially urgent in staying away from presumptions about jobs and assumptions. In a little family, where every part's commitment is essential, suspicions can prompt neglected assumptions and expected clashes. All things being equal, cultivating a culture of open correspondence permits relatives to communicate their necessities, arrange liabilities, and by and large shape the family's needs.

Besides, correspondence assumes an imperative part in imparting a feeling of shared liability and an aggregate character. Relatives who effectively take part in discussions about their jobs and commitments are bound to foster a common vision for the family's prosperity. This common vision turns into a directing power in navigation and builds up the possibility that obligations are not individual weights but rather shared responsibilities.

Difficulties and Systems for Powerful Obligation Dissemination:

While the little family setting offers benefits as far as flexibility and close associations, it likewise presents remarkable difficulties in the conveyance of obligations. One test emerges from the potential for job over-burden, where certain relatives might feel overpowered by the assortment of jobs they are supposed to satisfy. This can be especially articulated for guardians shuffling work, childcare, and family obligations.

To address job over-burden, little families frequently utilize systems like undertaking prioritization, using time productively, and setting sensible assumptions. Recognizing that few out of every odd obligation requires prompt consideration and that looking for help from relatives or outer sources is adequate can relieve sensations of overpower.

Another test is the potential for job vagueness, where hazy assumptions lead to disarray and disappointment. To conquer this, little families can profit from laying out clear job assumptions through open discourse. Examining individual qualities, inclinations, and limits makes a mutual perspective of every part's commitments and guarantees that jobs line up with capacities and interests.

In circumstances where outer stressors, for example, monetary tensions or medical problems, influence the family, viable correspondence turns out to be considerably more basic. Little families might have to adjust jobs and obligations to explore these difficulties cooperatively, building up the strength of the nuclear family.

3.2 Illustration of how each member's role contributes to the family dynamic.

Inside the mind boggling dance of a relational peculiarity, every part expects an unmistakable job that adds to the amicable working and by and large prosperity of the unit. The familial embroidery is woven with the strings of different commitments, with every part having an imperative impact in establishing a supporting climate. In this investigation, we dig into the delineation of how every relative's job adds to the multifaceted and advancing elements inside the family setting.

Parental Jobs as Mainstays of Help:

The fundamental mainstays of the family structure are much of the time encapsulated by the parental jobs. Guardians, in their complex limits, act as suppliers, nurturers, guides, and good examples. The special commitments of each parent make a reasonable and steady groundwork whereupon the relational peculiarity is constructed.

The job of a mother, customarily connected with sustaining and consistent encouragement, is crucial in making a warm and caring climate inside the family.

From overseeing everyday schedules to offering compassionate tuning in, a mother's job is described by a natural capacity to encourage close to home associations. In the midst of festivity and difficulty the same, a mother's presence turns into a consistent anchor, giving solace and direction.

On the other hand, the job of a dad is frequently connected to the arrangement of material and monetary help, as well as granting a feeling of discipline and design. Fathers add to the relational intricacy by offering steadiness, direction, and a feeling that all is well with the world. Their association in dynamic cycles and support of independence in youngsters' advancement enhance the general family experience.

The cooperative energy between parental jobs is a critical determinant of the family's versatility. While each parent might have unmistakable obligations, compelling correspondence and joint effort guarantee that their jobs complete one another, establishing a durable and supporting climate for the whole family.

Youngsters' Jobs in Shaping the Family Account:

Youngsters, in their one of a kind jobs inside the family, add to the lively story of development, learning, and shared encounters. As beneficiaries of care and direction, youngsters additionally effectively partake in deeply shaping the relational peculiarity by bringing their distinction and viewpoints into the overlay.

In the early years, youngsters' jobs are based on getting adoration, care, and instructive direction from their folks. Nonetheless, as they develop, their jobs advance to incorporate liabilities like scholastic pursuits, family tasks, and adding to dynamic cycles. The progress from being exclusively beneficiaries to dynamic patrons is an essential stage in the relational peculiarity.

The job of a youngster as a student and safeguard of family values is instrumental in significantly shaping the family's personality. Through their cooperations with guardians and kin, kids incorporate social standards, virtues, and rules that structure the underpinning of the family's conviction framework. The inquiries they pose, the difficulties they present, and the interest they bring add to a dynamic and developing family story.

In addition, youngsters frequently become the impetuses for shared encounters, from family excursions to festivities and achievements. Their jobs as initiators of bliss, chuckling, and suddenness infuse essentialness into the relational peculiarity. The family's versatility to youngsters' changing requirements and their developing jobs is demonstrative of a responsive and strong family structure.

Kin as Friends and Co-Guides:

The jobs expected by kin inside the family are portrayed by friendship, shared encounters, and the improvement of a novel bond that reaches out past the parental domain. Kin assume different parts, filling in as friends, mates, and co-guides in the excursion of familial associations.

The kin relationship frequently includes a sensitive harmony between help and brotherhood. While kin elements might incorporate snapshots of contention and rivalry, the general job is one of common help and understanding. Kin, through shared encounters and the special comprehension they have of one another, become associates in exploring the intricacies of day to day life.

In their jobs as close companions and comrades, kin add to the profound scene of the family. The common recollections, inside jokes, and a feeling of shared history make a familial embroidery woven with the strings of kin bonds. As people develop and set out on their particular processes, the kin relationship turns into a consistent, giving a wellspring of congruity and association.

Besides, the jobs of kin reach out to their effect on one another's self-improvement. The elements of mentorship, impact, and shared learning add to the wealth of their jobs. Kin frequently act as mirrors, mirroring each other's assets and regions for development. The capacity to explore clashes, share liabilities, and commend each other's accomplishments encourages a feeling of fortitude that reinforces the general relational intricacy.

More distant family Individuals and the Embroidery of Help:

Past the close nuclear family, more distant family individuals assume particular parts that add to the more extensive embroidered artwork of help and interconnectedness. Grandparents, aunties, uncles, and cousins bring extra layers of involvement, astuteness, and connections that enhance the relational intricacy.

The jobs of grandparents, frequently portrayed by their abundance of life encounters, incorporate filling in as vaults of familial history and social practices. Grandparents add to the relational intricacy by offering a feeling of progression and a scaffold to generational information. Their jobs as narrators, coaches, and wellsprings of unrestricted love make a multi-generational aspect inside the family.

Aunties and uncles, in their jobs as more distant family individuals, act as extra wellsprings of help and direction. They might assume parts much the same as guides, offering points of view past the close family circle. The connections shaped with aunties and uncles add to the variety of familial associations, encouraging a feeling of inclusivity and having a place.

Cousins, frequently viewed as underlying companions, add to the relational intricacy by giving friendship and shared encounters. The jobs of cousins include shared play, common help, and the making of bonds that stretch out across ages. As people develop, the jobs of cousins advance into kinships that add to the wealth of the family account.

The reconciliation of more distant family jobs into the relational peculiarity requires compelling correspondence and a receptiveness to different viewpoints. The capacity to use the qualities and commitments of more distant family individuals makes an encouraging group of people that upgrades the family's versatility and flexibility.

Versatility in Developing Family Jobs:

One of the principal traits of a sound relational intricacy is its versatility to developing jobs as conditions change. The jobs inside a family are not static; they shift in light of life altering situations, individual development, and outside factors. The family's capacity to embrace and adjust to these progressions adds to its general prosperity.

For example, as youngsters progress through various formative stages, the jobs of guardians advance to address evolving issues. The shift from youth to puberty, with its unmistakable difficulties and open doors, expects guardians to change their jobs as suppliers of direction, teachers, and daily encouragement. Essentially, the change of kids into adulthood prompts a reexamination of parental jobs, underscoring mentorship, joint effort, and shared independent direction.

Life altering situations, for example, profession changes, movements, or wellbeing challenges likewise require a reconsideration of jobs inside the family. The flexibility to these progressions includes open correspondence, common help, and a common obligation to exploring difficulties together. The versatility of the relational peculiarity lies in its capacity to weather conditions storms, embrace development, and adjust jobs to line up with the advancing necessities of every part.

The flexibility isn't restricted to the close family yet stretches out to the coordination of new relatives through marriage, associations, or different types of familial development. The jobs of parents in law, step-guardians, and different increases to the nuclear family require a cognizant work to encourage inclusivity, recognize assorted viewpoints, and make a feeling of having a place.

Compelling Correspondence as an Impetus for Family Jobs:

At the core of every relative's commitment to the unique lies the impetus of viable correspondence. The capacity to communicate needs, share viewpoints, and take part in open exchange shapes the foundation of a sound relational peculiarity. Correspondence fills in as the course through what jobs are perceived, arranged, and adjusted in light of evolving conditions.

Family gatherings, whether formal or casual, give a stage to examining jobs, obligations, and the general heading of the family. Straightforward correspondence about assumptions, difficulties, and goals makes a mutual perspective among relatives. It cultivates a culture of coordinated effort, where every part feels appreciated, esteemed, and enabled to add to the family's prosperity.

Notwithstanding verbal correspondence, non-verbal signals likewise assume a huge part in relational peculiarities. Tokens of fondness, articulations of compassion, and shared exercises add to a nuanced comprehension of every relative's personal state and needs. The capacity to adjust to non-verbal correspondence improves the responsiveness and attachment of the nuclear family.

Powerful correspondence turns out to be especially essential during seasons of contention or conflict. The jobs of arbiter, attentive person, and sympathetic communicator come to the very front in settling clashes and encouraging comprehension. The obligation to a correspondence style that focuses on regard, approval, and the affirmation of different points of view fortifies the connections between relatives.

Shared Customs and Ceremonies:

The jobs of relatives are likewise communicated and supported through shared customs and ceremonies. These ceremonies, whether day to day schedules, festivities, or yearly occasions, add to the relational peculiarity by making a feeling of progression, personality, and shared encounters.

Day to day ceremonies, like family feasts or sleep time schedules, act as any open doors for association and shared minutes. The jobs of guardians, narrators, and sidekicks are ordered in these ordinary customs, adding to a feeling of business as usual and steadiness inside the relational peculiarity. The consistency of these ceremonies supports the jobs of every relative and encourages a feeling of having a place.

Festivities and customs mark critical achievements in the family account. The jobs of organizers, coordinators, and members come to the front in the arrangement of birthday events, occasions, and extraordinary events. These common encounters add to the aggregate memory of the family, making an embroidery woven with the strings of delight, chuckling, and shared customs.

The meaning of customs isn't restricted to glad events however reaches out to seasons of misfortune or challenge. The jobs of blanket, ally, and flexibility manufacturer are communicated in the common ceremonies of grieving, reflection, and recuperating. By exploring both euphoric and testing minutes through shared customs, relatives add to the flexibility and strength of the nuclear family.

In the unpredictable movement of relational peculiarities, every part expects a novel job that adds to the aggregate prosperity and story of the unit. From parental jobs as mainstays of help to the developing jobs of kids, kin, and more distant family individuals, every individual meshes their string into the familial woven artwork.

The flexibility of jobs because of life altering situations, compelling correspondence as an impetus for understanding, and the support of jobs through shared customs all assume vital parts in the strength of the relational peculiarity. It is inside this exchange of assorted jobs, each contributing its remarkable tint to the material of everyday life, that the genuine substance of familial associations is uncovered.

As relatives explore the recurring patterns of life, their jobs interweave, making a rich and nuanced story that mirrors the qualities, challenges, and shared encounters of the nuclear family. In embracing the meaning of every job, encouraging open correspondence, and respecting shared customs, families make an embroidery woven with the strings of affection, association, and the getting through bonds that characterize the embodiment of familial connections.

3.3 Reflection on the balance between individuality and shared duties.

At the core of familial congruity lies a sensitive dance among independence and shared obligations, a nuanced transaction that characterizes the balance inside the relational peculiarity. As people exist together inside the cozy limits of a nuclear family, each with their exceptional personality, desires, and limits, the test emerges in orchestrating these distinctions with aggregate liabilities. In this reflection, we dig into the complexities of adjusting distinction and shared obligations inside the family, investigating how this harmony shapes connections, supports self-improvement, and adds to the general prosperity of the familial unit.

Embracing Distinction inside the Family:

The underpinning of a flourishing relational peculiarity is based upon the acknowledgment and festivity of independence. Every relative, from guardians to youngsters and broadened family members, brings a special arrangement of characteristics, gifts, and viewpoints that improve the aggregate embroidery. Embracing independence inside the family setting includes recognizing and esteeming these distinctions as necessary parts of the familial character.

Guardians, as the designers of the family ethos, assume a pivotal part in cultivating a climate that permits every kid to unfurl their distinction. Sustaining a kid's advantages, supporting their desires, and empowering the declaration of their valid selves add to the improvement of a solid feeling of individual personality. This accentuation on distinction reaches out to the affirmation of assorted qualities, learning styles, and character attributes among kin.

In equal, the jobs of kin inside the family give amazing open doors to the articulation and investigation of uniqueness. While familial securities make a common history and association, the acknowledgment of every kin's special personality is essential in cultivating a feeling of independence and self-revelation. The family turns into a strong scenery against which individual individuals can unfurl their true capacity, seek after private interests, and explore their excursion of self-disclosure.

Shared Obligations as a String of Association:

As independence shapes the lively tones inside the familial material, shared obligations arise as the strings that mesh these different components into a strong and useful entirety. The idea of shared obligations infers an aggregate obligation to obligations that add to the prosperity of the nuclear family. These obligations range a range, including family tasks, independent direction, everyday encouragement, and the general organization of day to day existence.

Guardians, as the essential stewards of the family, frequently start and guide the circulation of shared obligations. Family obligations, like cooking, cleaning, and sorting out, are shared to impart a feeling of coordinated effort and shared proprietorship. Dynamic cycles include the aggregate contribution of relatives, cultivating a vote based approach that values different viewpoints and guarantees that every part's voice is heard.

Kids, as well, partake in shared obligations inside the family, adding to mature fitting errands and continuously taking on additional obligations as they develop. The jobs they expect, whether in assisting with errands or partaking in family conversations, impart a feeling of responsibility and a comprehension that the working of the family is an aggregate undertaking. The harmony between individual independence and shared liabilities turns into a developmental part of their formative process.

Exploring the Strains:

While the ideal is to work out some kind of harmony among uniqueness and shared obligations, the truth frequently presents pressures and difficulties. Individual yearnings might conflict with aggregate needs, individual limits might be tried in the domain of shared liabilities, and varying assumptions can make contact inside the familial space. Exploring these pressures requires a sensitive dance of correspondence, adaptability, and a common obligation to seeing each other's viewpoints.

One normal wellspring of strain emerges from the contrasting assumptions put on individual relatives. While some might flourish in jobs that include more noticeable commitments, others might favor calmer types of help or express their consideration through profound means. The test lies in perceiving and regarding these different methodologies, guaranteeing that the dispersion of shared obligations obliges the one of a kind qualities and inclinations of every relative.

Correspondence turns into a key part in exploring these strains. Transparent discussions about individual requirements, limits, and yearnings make an establishment for understanding. Explaining assumptions and arranging jobs inside the family setting permit relatives to verbalize their singular needs while aggregately pursuing shared objectives.

Furthermore, adaptability is foremost in keeping up with balance. The developing idea of individual personalities and outside conditions requires a readiness to adjust jobs and assumptions. This flexibility isn't a split the difference of distinction yet an acknowledgment that the harmony between private desires and shared obligations is dynamic and dependent upon future developments.

Encouraging Self-improvement inside Shared Spaces:

A vital part of the harmony among uniqueness and shared obligations is the job it plays in encouraging self-awareness inside shared spaces. The nuclear family, as a microcosm of society, fills in as a basic climate where people learn, advance, and foster a healthy identity. The interchange between self-improvement and shared liabilities establishes a climate that supports the comprehensive advancement of every relative.

Youngsters, specifically, go through critical periods of development inside the familial setting. The harmony between individual investigation and shared obligations permits them to develop a feeling of organization and obligation. Support in shared liabilities, for example, errands or dynamic cycles, adds to the advancement of fundamental abilities, including using time effectively, cooperation, and critical thinking.

Guardians, as well, experience self-improvement inside the relational peculiarity. Adjusting individual pursuits, whether expert or individual, with shared liabilities requires a ceaseless course of self-disclosure and transformation. The capacity to coordinate self-awareness with familial responsibilities makes a model for youngsters, representing the significance of deep rooted learning and the quest for individual interests inside the setting of aggregate liabilities.

Kin, through their connections and shared encounters, add to one another's self-awareness. The jobs they expect as mates, allies, and in some cases challengers establish a powerful climate where people figure out how to explore connections, construct strength, and value the variety of points of view inside the familial unit.

Developing a Feeling of Aggregate Reason:

The sensitive harmony among distinction and shared obligations is much of the time moored it could be said of aggregate reason that rises above individual yearnings. Laying out and building up a common vision for the nuclear family makes a strong structure inside which individual individuals can adjust their own objectives to more extensive familial goals. This aggregate reason turns into a directing power that shapes the conveyance of obligations and illuminates dynamic cycles.

The verbalization of a common vision frequently includes family conversations where individuals express their qualities, objectives, and desires. These conversations make a common story that underlines the meaning of every part's commitment to the general prosperity of the family. The jobs expected inside this setting are not seen as segregated obligations but rather as interconnected strings that weave the family account.

In circumstances where strains emerge, getting back to this feeling of aggregate reason fills in as a compass for reorientation. Returning to shared values, objectives, and the familial vision permits relatives to recalibrate their jobs and needs. The aggregate reason turns into a wellspring of motivation, cultivating a feeling of solidarity and versatility even with difficulties.

Cultivating Sympathy and Understanding:

A foundation in the journey for balance among singularity and shared obligations is the development of sympathy and figuring out inside the familial space. Every relative brings a one of a kind arrangement of encounters, viewpoints, and difficulties. Encouraging a climate where people effectively try to comprehend and understand each other's real factors makes an establishment for agreeable conjunction.

Sympathy includes perceiving and approving the feelings, requirements, and yearnings of others inside the family. Understanding that every relative might explore their own arrangement of difficulties, yearnings, and wants adds to a culture of sympathy and backing. The jobs expected inside the family, hence, become errands to satisfy as well as any open doors to broaden sympathy and care.

Powerful correspondence assumes a urgent part in sustaining sympathy and understanding. Empowering relatives to communicate their sentiments, articulate their necessities, and offer their points of view encourages an environment of receptiveness. The capacity to effectively tune in, without judgment, permits relatives to acquire bits of knowledge into one another's encounters, encouraging a more profound comprehension of the intricacies that shape individual personalities.

The Effect on Relationship Elements:

The harmony among independence and shared obligations fundamentally impacts the elements of connections inside the family. Parental connections, kin bonds, and associations with more distant family individuals are totally formed by the sensitive harmony between individual independence and aggregate liabilities.

Parental connections, grounded in a common comprehension of one another's distinction and a common obligation to nurturing, flourish when there is an equilibrium in jobs and obligations. The capacity of guardians to explore individual goals while effectively taking part in shared obligations makes a model of organization and coordinated effort.

This equilibrium adds to the close to home prosperity of the two guardians and reinforces the establishment whereupon the family is assembled.

Kin connections, frequently portrayed by a blend of fellowship and periodic clash, benefit from an equilibrium that recognizes and celebrates individual contrasts. The jobs of kin as sidekicks and co-pilots become more agreeable when there is a comprehension of one another's novel characters and a common obligation to shared help. The equilibrium considers the development of solid, strong bonds that stretch out past youth into adulthood.

More distant family connections, impacted by the harmony among singularity and shared obligations, are portrayed by a feeling of interconnectedness. At the point when relatives get it and value each other's singular commitments and shared liabilities, a strong organization arises. The jobs expected inside this drawn out familial setting add to the wealth of connections, cultivating a feeling of having a place and progression.

Difficulties and Procedures for Equilibrium:

While the quest for balance among distinction and shared obligations is optimistic, it isn't without its difficulties. Perceiving and exploring these difficulties requires a proactive methodology, grounded in compelling correspondence, adaptability, and a common obligation to shared understanding.

One test emerges from outer impacts, for example, cultural assumptions or social standards, that might force inflexible assumptions on individual jobs inside the family. Breaking liberated from these outer tensions and making a familial space where jobs are arranged in light of individual limits and goals is vital. Open discussions about outside assumptions and the family's obligation to making its exceptional personality can assist with moderating these difficulties.

Another test comes from moving needs and advancing life stages. As people develop, seek after instruction, leave on professions, or experience huge life altering situations, the harmony between individual desires and shared liabilities might be upset. Exploring these changes requires a readiness to adjust jobs, reevaluate needs, and impart transparently about the changing elements inside the family.

Procedures for keeping up with balance include the development of a family culture that focuses on open correspondence and adaptability. Laying out ordinary family gatherings where jobs and obligations are examined, assumptions are explained, and challenges are tended to makes a stage for continuous discourse. This proactive methodology permits relatives to cooperatively shape the harmony among distinction and shared obligations.

Also, the job of appreciation and affirmation couldn't possibly be more significant. Perceiving and offering thanks for every relative's commitments, whether individual accomplishments or shared liabilities, cultivates a positive and strong climate.

The affirmation of endeavors and the festival of achievements add to a culture where every part feels esteemed and roused to take part in the familial space effectively.

In the perplexing dance of familial elements, the harmony among uniqueness and shared obligations arises as a focal subject that shapes connections, sustains self-improvement, and adds to the general prosperity of the nuclear family. Embracing singularity inside the family includes perceiving and praising the remarkable characteristics and desires of every relative. Shared obligations, then again, structure the strings that mesh these singularities into a firm and useful entire, making a feeling of aggregate reason.

The pressures that emerge in exploring this equilibrium become open doors for development, correspondence, and a more profound comprehension of one another's real factors. The nuclear family, as a microcosm of society, turns into a pot where people figure out how to communicate their valid selves while effectively taking part in the common obligations that add to the aggregate prosperity.

At last, the quest for balance among uniqueness and shared obligations is a dynamic and progressing process. It requires versatility, compelling correspondence, and a pledge to cultivating a familial space where every part feels seen, heard, and esteemed. In striking this sensitive harmony, families establish an amicable climate where the lavishness of individual personalities upgrades the aggregate strength and versatility of the familial unit. The interchange among independence and shared obligations turns into a demonstration of the getting through bonds that characterize the substance of familial connections.

Chapter 4

"Strength in Simplicity"

In the multifaceted embroidery of current life, where intricacy frequently rules, the idea of "Solidarity in Straightforwardness" arises as a signal of clearness and strength. An affirmation power and significance can be seen as in the direct, the cleaned up, and the fundamental parts of presence. This reflection investigates the diverse components of "Solidarity in Effortlessness," disentangling how this way of thinking pervades different aspects of our lives, from individual prosperity to cultural designs.

Individual Prosperity:

At its center, the idea of "Solidarity in Effortlessness" advocates for a re-visitation of fundamentals chasing individual prosperity. In a world immersed with consistent improvements and requests, straightforwardness turns into a wellspring of comfort and equilibrium. This straightforwardness isn't a dismissal of intricacy however a purposeful decision to distil life to its fundamental components, encouraging a feeling of clearness and concentration.

The straightforwardness in day to day schedules and propensities can be a groundbreaking power in advancing mental and profound prosperity. Embracing a moderate way to deal with individual spaces, cleaning up the brain, and working on everyday ceremonies can establish a climate helpful for peacefulness and reflection. The force of straightforwardness lies in its capacity to lessen the psychological commotion, permitting people to legitimately associate with their viewpoints and feelings more.

Also, "Strength in Effortlessness" reaches out to the domain of way of life decisions. Improving on dietary propensities, embracing a less materialistic way to deal with assets, and focusing on encounters over belongings are features of a less complex way of life that add to a more significant feeling of satisfaction. Chasing individual prosperity, effortlessness turns into a core value, empowering people to zero in on the main thing and dispose of the unessential.

Care and Present Second Mindfulness:

The act of care exemplifies the pith of "Solidarity in Straightforwardness." Care, established in the development of present second mindfulness, urges people to draw in with life in its easiest structure - the present time and place. By focusing on the present, people can explore the intricacies of thought and feeling with more prominent lucidity and composure.

Care rehearses, like contemplation and careful breathing, epitomize the strength tracked down in straightforwardness. These practices distil the craft of mindfulness to its quintessence, encouraging an association with the current second that is liberated from the weights of remorseful thoughts or future tensions. The straightforwardness of zeroing in on one's breath or noticing contemplations without judgment turns into a powerful wellspring of inward strength and versatility.

With regards to day to day existence, the use of care reaches out to straightforward demonstrations like relishing a dinner, appreciating nature, or completely captivating in discussions. These apparently standard minutes, when drawn nearer with careful presence, uncover their uncommon extravagance. The strength got from such effortlessness lies in the significant association with the profundity and excellence innate in the texture of regular daily existence.

Natural Stewardship:

The standard of "Solidarity in Straightforwardness" tracks down reverberation in the domain of ecological stewardship. In a world wrestling with the outcomes of overconsumption and natural corruption, effortlessness turns into a strong partner in cultivating manageable practices. The comprehension that less can for sure be more penetrates ways to deal with utilization, squander decrease, and the by and large natural impression.

Feasible living hugs the effortlessness of careful utilization - a conscious decision to focus on higher standards without compromise, sturdiness over superfluity. This change in context challenges the unavoidable culture of overabundance, welcoming people to think about the natural effect of their decisions. The strength in this effortlessness lies in the aggregate force of careful shoppers to impact ventures, drive development, and add to a more practical future.

Moderation, as an exemplification of straightforwardness, offers a convincing structure for natural stewardship. The intentional decrease of assets, the accentuation on usefulness, and the dismissal of superfluous realism line up with the ethos of manageability. In embracing a moderate way of life, people add to a culture that esteems the life span of products, diminishes squander, and advances a more cognizant relationship with the climate.

Connections and Association:

In the unpredictable snare of human connections, "Strength in Straightforwardness" appears as an extraordinary power. The effortlessness in correspondence, portrayed by genuineness and weakness, frames the bedrock of significant associations. Deprived of misrepresentation and intricacy, certified human communications become a wellspring of solidarity and close to home versatility.

The effortlessness in connections likewise includes a cognizant decision to focus on higher standards without ever compromising. Developing a little circle of profound associations cultivates a feeling of closeness and basic encouragement. In this present reality where informal communities can become rambling and shallow, the strength of straightforwardness lies in the profundity of association as opposed to the broadness of colleagues.

Also, "Strength in Straightforwardness" challenges cultural assumptions and standards encompassing connections. The effortlessness in characterizing one's connections, whether familial, non-romantic, or heartfelt, includes genuineness in communicating needs and limits. The strength in this effortlessness is the making of connections grounded in shared understanding and regard, unburdened by ridiculous assumptions or cultural tensions.

Proficient Pursuits and Imagination:

In the domain of expert pursuits, the rule of "Solidarity in Effortlessness" reshapes the account around progress and efficiency. The effortlessness in objective setting, zeroing in on a couple of key targets with lucidity and devotion, can prompt more effective results. This purposeful straightforwardness counters the common culture of performing various tasks and steady hecticness, permitting people to channel their energy into attempts that line up with their qualities and needs.

Imagination, as well, flourishes in the hug of straightforwardness. The strength of straightforwardness in the innovative strategy lies in refining complex thoughts into their fundamental parts.

Whether in craftsmanship, plan, composing, or development, the force of straightforwardness is obvious in the tastefulness and clearness of the eventual outcome. Stripping away superfluous intricacy permits the embodiment of inventiveness to radiate through.

In proficient settings, the effortlessness of powerful correspondence turns into a foundation of cooperation and achievement. The strength in clear, compact correspondence lies in its capacity to connect holes, adjust groups, and encourage a mutual perspective of objectives. Effortlessness in initiative includes an emphasis on fundamental beliefs, straightforward correspondence, and an accentuation on enabling people to seriously contribute.

Social and Philosophical Points of view:

"Social moderation" encapsulates the ethos of "Solidarity in Straightforwardness" with regards to cultural qualities and social points of view. This idea challenges the thought that advancement and thriving are intrinsically attached to material collection and lavishness. All things considered, social moderation recommends that strength and satisfaction can be tracked down in the straightforwardness of shared encounters, local area associations, and an emphasis on prosperity.

Societies that embrace effortlessness frequently focus on connections, collective prosperity, and an amicable conjunction with nature. The strength in this social effortlessness lies in the versatility of networks, the protection of customs, and the maintainable practices that persevere over the long run. The dismissal of unreasonable commercialization turns into an assertion of social character grounded in values past material riches.

Logically, "Strength in Effortlessness" lines up with different ways of thinking that underline the quest for a significant life over the collection of assets. Ways of thinking, for example, Emotionlessness and certain Eastern methods of reasoning backer for straightforwardness as a pathway to internal harmony and happiness. The strength in embracing these philosophical viewpoints lies in the freedom from the quest for outside approvals and the development of a persevering through feeling of satisfaction.

Versatility in Affliction:

The strength found in effortlessness is maybe most obvious in the midst of misfortune. When confronted with difficulties, the straightforwardness of fundamental beliefs, significant connections, and an emphasis on basics turns into a wellspring of flexibility. In difficulty, people and networks frequently find a natural capacity to persevere and adjust by embracing the strength innate in effortlessness.

The effortlessness of reaction to difficulty includes an unmistakable looked at evaluation of needs and a purposeful spotlight on the main thing. Even with surprising emergencies, the strength in straightforwardness lies in the capacity to turn, change, and track down comfort in the key parts of life - love, association, and a feeling of direction.

This straightforwardness isn't a forswearing of intricacy yet an essential reaction that slices through the commotion and jam the center of one's flexibility.

Moreover, the effortlessness of appreciation turns into an incredible asset in exploring difficulty. Recognizing and valuing the little, ordinary endowments encourages a positive outlook that adds to close to home prosperity. The strength in straightforwardness during provoking times lies in the capacity to track down snapshots of excellence, association, and significance even in the midst of affliction.

4.1 Exploration of the simplicity that characterizes the family's lifestyle.

In the core of familial elements, the investigation of effortlessness discloses an embroidery woven with strings of validness, association, and reason. The family's way of life, described by a guarantee to the fundamental, cultivates a climate where the extravagance of human connections becomes the dominant focal point. In this investigation, we dive into the different components of effortlessness inside the family, from everyday schedules to shared encounters, and think about how this obligation to the simple shapes the family's character and prosperity.

Day to day Schedules and Ceremonies:

At the center of the family's effortlessness lies the intentional plan of everyday schedules and ceremonies that underline association and shared encounters. The wake-up routine of breakfast together, the common obligations of everyday errands, and the night schedule of family time are ordinary undertakings as well as deliberate demonstrations that anchor the family one might say of harmony.

In the straightforwardness of day to day schedules, the family finds a musicality that rises above the rushed speed of present day life. The demonstration of sharing feasts turns into a sacrosanct custom, when relatives meet up to support their bodies as well as their bonds. The straightforwardness of preparing the table, sharing stories, and taking part in veritable discussions makes a space where the pith of familial association prospers.

The purposeful designation of jobs and obligations inside day to day schedules adds to the proficiency and amicability of the nuclear family. Every part's commitment, whether in planning dinners, keeping up with the home, or really focusing on more youthful kin, turns into a string in the complex embroidery of shared liabilities. This effortlessness in division of work cultivates a cooperative soul, where each undertaking, regardless of how little, is esteemed as a commitment to the aggregate prosperity.

Moderation and the Family Space:

The family's obligation to straightforwardness stretches out to the actual space they occupy. Moderation, as a core value, shapes the climate into a shelter of serenity and usefulness.

The intentional decision to shun overabundance and focus on significant belongings makes a space where each thing fills a need and holds importance.

In the straightforwardness of the family space, there is a deliberate work to clean up and establish a climate that supports a feeling of quiet. The common living spaces, decorated with painstakingly picked goods and significant curios, become an impression of the family's qualities. This deliberate effortlessness in the actual environmental elements adds to a feeling of request, encouraging a space where connections can prosper without the interruptions of material overabundance.

The standards of moderation likewise reach out to the family's way to deal with commercialization. Rather than surrendering to the tensions of steady securing, the family embraces a careful and deliberate way to deal with buys. This straightforwardness in utilization diminishes the family's environmental impression as well as builds up the upsides of appreciation and happiness over material gathering.

Turned off and Quality Time:

In a world overwhelmed by screens and computerized interruptions, the family's obligation to straightforwardness is clear in their purposeful decision to turn off and focus on quality time. The straightforwardness of nights spent without the interruption of electronic gadgets turns into a period for veritable association. Whether took part in narrating, playing prepackaged games, or essentially sharing giggling, the family esteems the straightforwardness of these minutes that structure the woven artwork of shared recollections.

The deliberate decision to restrict screen time isn't a dismissal of innovation yet an acknowledgment of the requirement for balance. By embracing the effortlessness of innovation free minutes, the family establishes a climate where up close and personal communications outweigh everything else. This purposeful turning off turns into a wellspring of solidarity, encouraging correspondence, sympathy, and a more profound comprehension of every relative's novel character.

Quality time additionally stretches out past the limits of the home. The family's obligation to straightforwardness includes the deliberate formation of encounters over belongings. Whether it's an end of the week climb, a visit to a nearby gallery, or a basic excursion in the recreation area, the family tracks down strength in the effortlessness of shared encounters. These minutes become the structure blocks of a common story, making an embroidery woven with strings of experience, disclosure, and happiness.

Monetary Effortlessness and Values-Based Living:

The family's obligation to effortlessness is in many cases reflected in their way to deal with monetary issues.

Rather than surrendering to the tensions of industrialism and the quest for material riches, the family embraces a qualities based way to deal with living. This effortlessness in monetary decisions includes adjusting spending to basic beliefs and needs.

The family's monetary effortlessness is described by purposeful planning, focusing on needs over needs, and settling on decisions that mirror their qualities. This deliberate living requires an insightful thought of the effect of monetary choices on the general prosperity of the family. The straightforwardness lies in the arrangement of monetary decisions with the family's yearnings for a significant and deliberate life.

Also, the family's monetary straightforwardness reaches out to the development of monetary education inside the family. Open discussions about cash, investment funds, and monetary objectives become indispensable parts of the family's qualities based living. This straightforwardness in monetary conversations encourages straightforwardness, joint effort, and a common feeling of obligation for the family's monetary prosperity.

Culinary Straightforwardness and Shared Sustenance:

The family's obligation to straightforwardness is many times exemplified in the culinary decisions that underscore shared sustenance and the delight of common feasts. The effortlessness in dinner readiness includes an emphasis on healthy fixings, shared cooking liabilities, and the delight of social event around the table for a common gala.

In the straightforwardness of culinary decisions, there is a cognizant work to focus on wellbeing and prosperity. The family esteems the demonstration of planning feasts together, changing the kitchen into a space for cooperation and shared innovativeness. This straightforwardness in the culinary space cultivates a feeling of association with the food, an appreciation for the work in question, and the delight of sharing a feast ready with affection.

The purposeful decision to focus on custom made feasts over cheap food or handled choices turns into a string in the embroidery of the family's obligation to prosperity. The straightforwardness of these culinary decisions adds to actual well-being as well as supports the upsides of shared liability, cooperation, and the delight of enjoying the kinds of a very much prepared feast together.

Effortlessness in Nurturing and Family Values:

The family's obligation to straightforwardness stretches out to the domain of nurturing, where deliberate decisions are made to cultivate a sustaining climate that values association over flawlessness. The effortlessness in nurturing includes an emphasis on basic beliefs like sympathy, correspondence, and shared regard. Rather than capitulating to cultural tensions or unreasonable assumptions, the family embraces the effortlessness of credible, values-driven nurturing.

In the effortlessness of nurturing, there is an affirmation that flawlessness isn't the objective. All things being equal, the family esteems the excursion of development, learning, and versatility. This deliberate straightforwardness in nurturing decisions permits every relative, the two guardians and kids, to communicate their credible selves and explore the intricacies of existence with a feeling of elegance.

The family's obligation to straightforwardness in nurturing likewise includes the deliberate development of the capacity to understand people on a profound level. Open correspondence, undivided attention, and the consolation of individual articulation become mainstays of the family's way to deal with sustaining close to home prosperity. This effortlessness in close to home association encourages a climate where every relative feels seen, heard, and esteemed.

Social Effortlessness and Customs:

Social effortlessness turns into an unmistakable string in the family's embroidery, winding around together customs, ceremonies, and a feeling of legacy. Rather than capitulating to outside pressures or the commodification of social practices, the family embraces the effortlessness of customs that hold individual importance and cultivate a feeling of having a place.

The deliberate development of social effortlessness includes an emphasis on shared ceremonies and festivities that interface the family to its social roots. Whether it's commending celebrations, partaking in far-reaching developments, or participating in customary practices, the family tracks down strength in the straightforwardness of these common social encounters. This deliberate living permits every relative to foster a profound appreciation for their social character.

Additionally, the family's obligation to social effortlessness includes the passing down of customs starting with one age then onto the next. The straightforwardness in the transmission of social qualities and practices turns into an approach to protecting a feeling of progression and association with the past. This purposeful living permits the family to explore the intricacies of a multicultural world with a solid feeling of social personality.

Instructive Straightforwardness and Deep rooted Learning:

In the domain of schooling, the family's obligation to effortlessness is reflected in a methodology that values long lasting learning, interest, and the quest for information for its characteristic worth. Rather than surrendering to outside pressures or the quest for instructive honors, the family embraces an effortlessness of direction that spins around the delight of learning.

Instructive effortlessness includes a climate where interest is supported, and the affection for learning turns into a long lasting sidekick.

The family esteems the effortlessness of investigating different subjects, participating in significant conversations, and encouraging a feeling of scholarly interest. This deliberate way to deal with training builds up the possibility that learning isn't a necessary evil however a consistent excursion.

Besides, the family's obligation to instructive effortlessness includes an acknowledgment of the different learning styles and goals of every relative. Rather than forcing inflexible assumptions, the family supports independence, self-revelation, and the quest for interests. This straightforwardness in instructive decisions cultivates a climate where every relative can unfurl their exceptional potential and add to the aggregate embroidery of information.

4.2 Examples of how a minimalist approach contributes to a close-knit atmosphere.

Chasing cultivating an affectionate environment, a moderate methodology turns into a strong and deliberate decision that pervades different features of life. The substance of moderation lies in improving and cleaning up, permitting the main thing to become the overwhelming focus. In this investigation, we dive into models showing how a moderate methodology adds to an affectionate air inside families, networks, and individual connections.

1. **Shared Spaces and Purposeful Plan:**

   A moderate way to deal with shared spaces inside a family or local area establishes the groundwork for an affectionate climate. The deliberate plan of living spaces includes cleaning up and zeroing in on the fundamental. Rather than being overpowered by overabundance assets, a moderate climate empowers straightforwardness, making open and welcoming spaces that encourage a feeling of fellowship.

   In a family setting, shared spaces, for example, the lounge or feasting region mirror the moderate ethos. Basic, utilitarian furnishings and cautiously organized style add to an environment of quiet and attachment. The deliberate plan of these common spaces urges relatives to accumulate, participate in discussions, and offer quality time without the interruptions of pointless mess.

2. **Smart Utilization and Careful Buys:**

   A moderate way to deal with utilization significantly affects connections inside a family or local area. Rather than capitulating to the tensions of realism, people embracing moderation make insightful and careful buys. This deliberate living lines up with the upsides of higher standards no matter what, empowering an emphasis on encounters and shared minutes over collecting assets.

In a family, this means a common obligation to careful utilization. The effortlessness of claiming just what is really important encourages a culture of appreciation and happiness. As relatives go with deliberate decisions about what to bring into their lives, there is an aggregate consciousness of the effect of each buy on the general prosperity of the family. This mutual perspective adds to an affectionate air grounded in shared values.

3. **Quality Time Over Material Belongings:**

A moderate methodology puts an exceptional on encounters over material belongings, underscoring the significance of value time spent together. In an affectionate family, this ethos appears in shared exercises, trips, and encounters that extend the connections between relatives. The effortlessness of picking encounters over gathering things turns into a wellspring of euphoria and association.

For instance, a moderate family could focus on an end of the week setting up camp outing, a nature climb, or a game night over gaining more belongings. These common encounters make enduring recollections and fortify the feeling of solidarity inside the family. The effortlessness of esteeming time together over material gathering adds to an affectionate air where the emphasis is on the extravagance of shared minutes.

4. **Smoothed out Correspondence and Profound Association:**

Moderation stretches out past actual belongings to the domain of correspondence and close to home association. In an affectionate environment, the effortlessness of smoothed out correspondence turns into a key component. Relatives rehearsing moderation in correspondence focus on lucidity, credibility, and undivided attention.

For example, the straightforwardness of communicating sentiments transparently and truly cultivates profound association inside the family. Rather than covering feelings or exploring through layers of intricacy, relatives embrace the straightforwardness that moderation in correspondence empowers. This deliberate methodology makes a climate where every part feels appreciated, comprehended, and esteemed.

5. **Cleaned up Timetables and Shared Liabilities:**

A moderate way to deal with using time productively contributes essentially to an affectionate air inside families. Improving on timetables and responsibilities takes into consideration greater quality time together. In an affectionate family, the straightforwardness of cleaned up plans implies purposefully cutting out minutes for shared exercises, discussions, and unwinding.

Besides, a moderate methodology reaches out to shared liabilities inside the family. Rather than overpowering every part with an overabundance of errands, there is a conscious work to smooth out liabilities, encouraging a feeling of cooperation and shared trouble. This straightforwardness in the dispersion of errands adds to an affectionate environment where relatives feel upheld and esteemed.

6. **Self-improvement and Aggregate Desires:**

Moderation urges people to zero in on self-improvement and satisfaction, lining up with their qualities and desires. In an affectionate family, this approach converts into an aggregate obligation to supporting every part's excursion of self-disclosure and self-awareness. The straightforwardness of empowering individual yearnings makes an environment of understanding and support.

For instance, in the event that one relative chooses to seek after an energy or leave on another vocation way, the moderate ethos inside the family upholds and praises this choice. There is an affirmation that self-awareness adds to the general prosperity of the nuclear family. The effortlessness of adjusting individual yearnings to aggregate qualities reinforces the bonds inside the family, cultivating an air of shared help.

7. **Ceremonies of Appreciation and Appreciation:**

A moderate methodology supports the act of appreciation and appreciation for what is available at the time. In an affectionate family, this straightforwardness in recognizing and praising the little delights of daily existence turns into a strong holding custom. Offering thanks for shared feasts, recognizing each other's commitments, and praising accomplishments cultivates a culture of energy and association.

For example, a moderate family could integrate a day to day or week by week custom of offering thanks. This straightforwardness in recognizing the wealth of the current second develops an affectionate air where relatives feel esteemed and appreciated. The demonstration of sharing appreciation turns into a bringing together string that reinforces the bonds inside the family.

8. **Adaptability and Flexibility:**

Moderation advances an adaptable and versatile mentality, empowering people to embrace change and explore vulnerabilities with strength. In an affectionate family, this effortlessness in approach converts into an aggregate capacity to adjust to developing conditions. The family turns into a strong unit that countenances difficulties together, tracking down strength in the straightforwardness of common help.

For instance, in the event that surprising changes happen, for example, a transition to another area or a change in relational peculiarities, the moderate methodology inside the family considers a smooth progress. The effortlessness of focusing on versatility over unbending schedules encourages an environment where relatives have a good sense of reassurance and upheld, even notwithstanding change.

9. **Careful Compromise:**

In affectionate families, clashes are unavoidable, however a moderate way to deal with compromise improves on the cycle and builds up the connections between relatives. The effortlessness of tending to clashes transparently and with an emphasis on goal instead of heightening makes an air of understanding and development.

For instance, rather than permitting irritating issues to wait, a moderate family could participate in transparent discussions to address clashes. The effortlessness of moving toward clashes with compassion and a common obligation to goal reinforces the family's solidarity. In this environment, clashes become open doors for development and improved seeing as opposed to wellsprings of division.

10. **Natural Awareness and Shared Values:**

A moderate way of life frequently lines up with ecological cognizance, underscoring supportability and capable utilization. In affectionate families, this common worth turns into a binding together power. The straightforwardness of going with eco-accommodating decisions by and large adds to a feeling of shared liability regarding the prosperity of the planet and people in the future.

For example, a moderate family could decide on maintainable practices like reusing, decreasing waste, and picking harmless to the ecosystem items. This common obligation to ecological cognizance turns into an impression of the family's qualities, adding to an affectionate environment where every part knows about their effect on the world and effectively takes part in going with positive decisions.

4.3 Reflection on finding strength in simplicity and shared values.

Finding strength in effortlessness and shared values is a significant excursion that rises above the shallow layers of current life, welcoming people and networks to rediscover the power intrinsic in the fundamental and the true. This reflection investigates the exchange among effortlessness and shared values, digging into the extraordinary effect of embracing a day to day existence grounded in center standards. From individual prosperity to the elements of connections and the more extensive cultural texture, the investigation of solidarity in straightforwardness enlightens a way towards versatility, association, and a more significant presence.

Individual Prosperity:

At the core of finding strength in effortlessness is the significant effect on private prosperity. In a world described by consistent commotion, requests, and interruptions, the effortlessness of purposeful living turns into a safe-haven for the brain, body, and soul. Stripping away the abundance and zeroing in on the fundamental permits people to reconnect with their guiding principle, goals, and the natural wellsprings of satisfaction.

Effortlessness in private prosperity includes a purposeful decision to focus on mental and profound wellbeing. Care rehearses, for example, contemplation and self-reflection, become instruments for exploring the intricacies of existence with lucidity and composure. The strength found in these basic practices lies in their capacity to develop a feeling of presence, establishing people in the extravagance of the current second.

Besides, the effortlessness of taking care of oneself turns into a foundation of individual prosperity. Embracing a moderate way to deal with way of life decisions, from diet to day to day schedules, includes focusing on higher standards no matter what. The strength in these decisions lies in their ability to cultivate a comprehensive feeling of health - sustaining the body with healthy food sources, taking part in active work, and encouraging soothing rest.

Shared values intensify the effect of individual prosperity, making an aggregate obligation to the rules that support a satisfying life. At the point when people inside a local area adjust their qualities, a feeling of common perspective arises, and the strength in this common establishment turns into a repository of help during both testing and euphoric times.

Association and Connections:

The effortlessness of shared values goes about as a strong impetus for significant associations inside connections. In the embroidery of human associations, shared values structure the strings that tight spot people, families, and networks together. These common standards become the language through which individuals figure out, regard, and backing each other.

In personal connections, the strength of straightforwardness lies in the legitimacy of shared values. Couples who adjust their center standards make a groundwork of trust, shared understanding, and close to home closeness. The effortlessness of shared values permits people to explore the intricacies of associations with a common compass, encouraging flexibility and a profound feeling of association.

Relational peculiarities are significantly affected by the straightforwardness of shared values. At the point when families on the whole hug a bunch of core values, they establish a climate where every part feels seen, heard, and esteemed. The strength in this common establishment becomes apparent during snapshots of festivity, difficulty, and the regular associations that shape the family story.

Inside people group, the straightforwardness of shared values turns into a binding together power that rises above individual contrasts. Whether in view of social, moral, or social standards, shared values make a shared view for different people to meet up. The strength in this solidarity lies in the capacity to pool assets, support aggregate drives, and make a versatile local area texture.

Flexibility in Affliction:

The strength found in straightforwardness and shared values is maybe most clear in the midst of misfortune. While confronting difficulties, whether on an individual or cultural level, people and networks moored in shared standards display a momentous limit with respect to strength. The effortlessness of a common worth framework turns into a directing light, giving lucidity and motivation in exploring fierce waters.

In private difficulties, the strength of effortlessness lies in the capacity to focus on the main thing. A moderate outlook permits people to shed the pointless weights and spotlight on the center rules that carry significance to their lives. The effortlessness of adjusting activities to values cultivates a feeling of direction that can bring people through the most obscure of times.

On a cultural level, the straightforwardness of shared values turns into an establishment for aggregate strength. Social orders that develop a feeling of solidarity in view of normal standards exhibit an ability to strike to weather conditions emergencies. The strength in this common flexibility lies in the cooperative reaction to challenges, the shared encouraging groups of people that arise, and the ability to adjust and modify.

Local area and Social Texture:

Networks woven together by shared values epitomize the strength tracked down in straightforwardness. The straightforwardness of aggregate reason turns into a main thrust for positive change, social union, and the production of a versatile social texture. At the point when people inside a local area share a guarantee to center standards, a feeling of having a place and interconnectedness prospers.

The strength in local area straightforwardness lies in the common obligation regarding the prosperity of its individuals. Whether it's through cooperative drives, encouraging groups of people, or public festivals, the straightforwardness of shared values makes a feeling of aggregate character and reason. This common establishment turns into an impetus for local area driven projects, social drives, and the development of a lively community life.

Despite cultural difficulties, the effortlessness of shared values turns into a foundation for social advancement. Developments based on standards like equity, correspondence, and ecological supportability gain strength from the effortlessness of their message. The common qualities go about as an energizing point for different people to meet up in quest for a shared objective, cultivating a feeling of fortitude and aggregate organization.

Ecological Stewardship:

The strength found in effortlessness reaches out to the domain of natural stewardship. A moderate way to deal with utilization, combined with shared values fixated on supportability, turns into a strong power for positive biological effect.

The effortlessness of cognizant decisions, like diminishing waste, saving assets, and embracing eco-accommodating practices, adds to a better planet.

People who embrace a moderate way of life frequently track down strength in the straightforwardness of lessening their natural impression. The deliberate decisions to consume carefully, reuse, and focus on maintainable items become an unmistakable articulation of imparted values to significant ramifications for the climate. The strength in this effortlessness lies in the aggregate effect of numerous people going with cognizant decisions that benefit the planet.

Networks and social orders that share ecological qualities enhance the strength tracked down in effortlessness. At the point when an aggregate obligation to biological prosperity is woven into the texture of a local area, drives for ecological preservation pick up speed. The straightforwardness of shared values changes into pragmatic activities, from local area tidy up endeavors to promotion for manageable approaches.

Monetary Decisions and Moral Living:

The effortlessness of shared values reaches out to financial decisions and moral living. People and networks that adjust their qualities to their monetary choices make an expanding influence that impacts businesses, market patterns, and cultural standards. The strength tracked down in straightforwardness here lies in the capacity to drive positive change through purposeful utilization and financial practices.

On an individual level, the effortlessness of moral living includes pursuing decisions that line up with one's qualities. Whether it's supporting fair exchange, picking economical items, or upholding for socially mindful organizations, the strength in these decisions lies in the possibility to make a more evenhanded and morally cognizant commercial center.

Networks that share a promise to moral living tackle the strength tracked down in straightforwardness to shape neighborhood economies. From supporting neighborhood organizations to advancing fair work rehearses, the effortlessness of shared values turns into a main thrust for financial decisions that focus on individuals and the planet. This common responsibility adds to the making of versatile, moral economies.

Social Personality and Shared Customs:

Social straightforwardness, established in shared values and customs, turns into a strong power for saving personality and encouraging intergenerational associations. At the point when a local area shares a guarantee to social standards, the strength in this effortlessness lies in the coherence of customs, the festival of legacy, and the protection of social character.

On a singular level, embracing social straightforwardness includes regarding and passing down customs that reflect shared values. The effortlessness of social practices turns into a wellspring of solidarity, interfacing people to their underlying foundations and giving a feeling of having a place. This purposeful living cultivates a rich embroidery of social personality that rises above ages.

In people group where social straightforwardness is embraced, shared customs become a foundation for solidarity and flexibility. The strength in this straightforwardness lies in the capacity to explore social variety while saving guiding principle. Social practices, customs, and festivities become strings that weave a common story, cultivating understanding and appreciation for the extravagance of variety.

Chapter 5

"Celebrating Unity"

Commending solidarity is a significant affirmation of the strength that arises when people, networks, and social orders meet up in mutual perspective and association. This reflection investigates the complex elements of solidarity, digging into the meaning of aggregate concordance, the force of shared values, and the extraordinary effect of praising the assorted strings that weave the embroidery of human life. From individual connections to worldwide networks, the festival of solidarity unfurls as a unique power that rises above divisions, encourages understanding, and develops a common feeling of having a place.

Amicability in Variety:

At the core of praising solidarity is the acknowledgment of the magnificence inborn in variety. Solidarity doesn't suggest consistency yet embraces the rich embroidered artwork of contrasts that portray humankind. In a world set apart by shifted societies, points of view, and foundations, the festival of solidarity includes a deliberate work to encourage concordance in variety.

The strength found in praising solidarity in the midst of variety lies in the capacity to wind around together the horde strings of human experience. At the point when people from various different backgrounds meet up, sharing their one of a kind stories, customs, and viewpoints, a mosaic of understanding arises.

This festival includes recognizing the extravagance that variety brings, destroying generalizations, and valuing the worth that every individual adds to the aggregate entirety.

Besides, commending solidarity in variety turns into a strong reaction to the difficulties of a globalized world. The intricacy of contemporary issues, from civil rights to ecological maintainability, requires an aggregate exertion that draws on the different qualities and viewpoints of people and networks. The festival of solidarity turns into a call to connect isolates, embrace contrasts, and work cooperatively towards an additional comprehensive and agreeable future.

Shared Values as the Establishment:

The festival of solidarity finds most profound roots in shared values rise above individual contrasts. At the point when people or networks adjust their standards and goals, a strong feeling of normal reason arises. Shared values become the bedrock whereupon solidarity is constructed, giving an establishment to joint effort, understanding, and aggregate activity.

In private connections, the festival of solidarity through shared values includes people meeting up with a common comprehension of center standards. Whether in kinships, associations, or familial bonds, the strength of solidarity lies in the common obligation to standards like trust, regard, and love. This festival turns into a wellspring of strength, supporting people through life's difficulties and encouraging a feeling of association that perseveres.

On a cultural level, the festival of solidarity through shared values adds to the development of networks limited by a typical ethos. At the point when people inside a local area embrace standards like equity, uniformity, and empathy, an aggregate personality arises. This festival includes the purposeful development of values that guide social connections, shape social standards, and add to the formation of a common story.

Sympathy and Understanding:

Fundamental to the festival of solidarity is the development of sympathy and understanding. These characteristics become spans that interface people and networks, encouraging a significant feeling of shared humankind. The festival of solidarity through sympathy includes the capacity to step into the shoes of others, to perceive and approve their encounters, and to construct associations in light of empathy.

In private connections, the festival of solidarity through compassion includes undivided attention, open correspondence, and a real craving to figure out the points of view of others. The strength in this festival lies in the capacity to explore contrasts with effortlessness, to see the value in the remarkable excursion of every person, and to fashion associations that rise above shallow divisions.

On a more extensive scale, the festival of solidarity through compassion turns into an impetus for social change. At the point when networks look to comprehend the encounters of minimized or mistreated gatherings, sympathy turns into a main impetus for backing, equity, and inclusivity. This festival includes destroying hindrances, testing fundamental imbalances, and pursuing a general public where the standards of sympathy and figuring out structure the groundwork of aggregate activities.

Cooperation and Aggregate Activity:

The festival of solidarity reaches out into the domain of cooperation and aggregate activity. At the point when people and networks join with a mutual perspective, the potential for extraordinary effect becomes unlimited. The strength found in commending solidarity through coordinated effort lies in the aggregate ability to address complex difficulties, impact positive change, and fabricate a superior future.

In private connections, the festival of solidarity through cooperation includes the quest for shared objectives working together. Whether it's a family cooperating to defeat snags or companions uniting for a common task, the strength in this festival lies in the collaboration of aggregate endeavors. Cooperation cultivates a feeling of shared accomplishment and builds up the connections between people.

On a cultural level, the festival of solidarity through aggregate activity turns into a strong power for social change. Developments that arise with a common vision, whether supporting for social equality, natural supportability, or compassionate causes, represent the strength in aggregate activity. The festival includes people meeting up, pooling their assets, and utilizing their aggregate voice to achieve foundational change.

Observing Social Legacy:

A dynamic part of praising solidarity is the affirmation and enthusiasm for social legacy. The assorted woven artwork of human societies, customs, and chronicles adds to the wealth of worldwide society. The festival of solidarity through social appreciation includes perceiving the worth of each social string and encouraging a climate where different legacies are praised, saved, and shared.

In private connections, the festival of solidarity through social appreciation includes a profound regard for one another's experiences. Whether people come from various social or ethnic foundations, the strength in this festival lies in the common acknowledgment and festivity of assorted legacies. It includes finding out about and taking part in one another's social works on, encouraging a climate of inclusivity and association.

On a more extensive scale, the festival of solidarity through social appreciation turns into a foundation for worldwide congruity.

At the point when social orders embrace the wealth of their multicultural scenes, commending customs, dialects, and customs, a common perspective arises. This festival includes the conservation of social legacy, the advancement of social trade, and the production of a worldwide local area that qualities and regards different characters.

Instructive Strengthening:

The festival of solidarity is complicatedly attached to instructive strengthening - the possibility that information and learning can be amazing assets for encouraging grasping, destroying biases, and building spans among people and networks. The strength in commending solidarity through schooling lies in its capability to separate hindrances, challenge generalizations, and make an additional educated and interconnected world.

In private connections, the festival of solidarity through instructive strengthening includes a promise to learning and development. Couples, families, and companions who take part in shared instructive pursuits, whether formal or casual, add to the strength of their bonds. The festival includes a shared interest in scholarly turn of events, encouraging a climate where people feel mentally animated and upheld.

On a cultural level, the festival of solidarity through instructive strengthening turns into a power for social advancement. Admittance to quality schooling for all, paying little mind to foundation, enables people to challenge predispositions, widen their viewpoints, and contribute genuinely to society. This festival includes the acknowledgment that a knowledgeable people is fundamental for building spans, encouraging exchange, and making a more fair world.

Worldwide Citizenship and Social Obligation:

Praising solidarity stretches out past individual connections and nearby networks to the idea of worldwide citizenship and social obligation. The strength in this festival lies in the affirmation that people, regardless of topographical limits, share an aggregate liability regarding the prosperity of the planet and its occupants.

In private connections, the festival of solidarity through worldwide citizenship includes a common obligation to social obligation. Couples and families who take part in altruism, volunteerism, or reasonable living practices epitomize the strength in this festival. It includes perceiving the interconnectedness of worldwide issues and making an aggregate move to add to positive change.

On a more extensive scale, the festival of solidarity through worldwide citizenship turns into a groundbreaking power for tending to worldwide difficulties. Developments that promoter for natural supportability, common freedoms, and compassionate causes represent the strength in aggregate worldwide activity. This festival includes people and networks perceiving their common obligation to make a world that values equity, uniformity, and natural stewardship.

Flexibility and Strength in Affliction:

A significant part of commending solidarity is its job in cultivating versatility and strength in the midst of difficulty. At the point when people and networks join even with difficulties, the festival turns into a demonstration of the human soul's ability to persevere, adjust, and arise more grounded. The strength in praising solidarity in the midst of misfortune lies in the common assurance to defeat snags and construct a stronger future.

In private connections, the festival of solidarity in the midst of affliction includes people supporting each other through challenges. Whether confronting wellbeing emergencies, monetary hardships, or individual difficulties, the strength in this festival lies in the common comprehension that people are in good company in their battles. The festival includes shared strength, a promise to enduring tempests together, and the conviction that difficulties can be extraordinary open doors for development.

On a cultural level, the festival of solidarity in the midst of misfortune turns into a strong power for aggregate flexibility. Networks that meet up in the result of catastrophic events, financial slumps, or different emergencies epitomize the strength in this festival. It includes the acknowledgment that common bonds, shared encouraging groups of people, and cooperative endeavors are fundamental for remaking and making a stronger society.

In the reflection on praising solidarity, a significant truth arises - that the strength tracked down in common perspective, understanding, and association can possibly change people, networks, and the world. The festival of solidarity includes deliberate endeavors to cultivate congruity in variety, line up with shared values, and embrace the wealth of human experience.

This festival stretches out into different features of human life - from individual connections and social appreciation to instructive strengthening, worldwide citizenship, and versatility in difficulty. The strength found in commending solidarity lies in its capacity to connect separates, destroy biases, and make an additional comprehensive and interconnected world.

As people and networks explore the intricacies of the cutting edge period, the festival of solidarity turns into a source of inspiration. It welcomes a reexamination of points of view, a promise to compassion and understanding, and an acknowledgment of the extraordinary effect that purposeful endeavors towards solidarity can have on private prosperity, connections, and the more extensive structure holding the system together. In the festival of solidarity, there is a significant affirmation of the common excursion, the interconnectedness of all mankind, and the potential for making a reality where variety is commended, contrasts are embraced, and solidarity turns into a strong power for positive change.

5.1 Showcase of the family's unique traditions and celebrations.

The embroidered artwork of everyday life is woven with strings of special practices and festivities, each strand adding to the rich story of shared encounters, esteems, and appreciated minutes. In this grandstand, we dive into the complex subtleties of a family's unmistakable practices and festivities, unwinding the layers that make their aggregate story genuinely extraordinary. From yearly ceremonies to achievement occasions, the family's remarkable embroidery is a demonstration of the force of shared traditions in encouraging association, character, and a feeling of having a place.

Yearly Customs:

At the core of the family's one of a kind embroidery are yearly customs that mark the progression of time and make a feeling of congruity. These practices become secures, establishing relatives in shared encounters that range ages. Whether it's the yearly family get-together, a merry occasion gathering, or a remarkable approach to honoring birthday celebrations, these customs act as touchpoints that unite the family.

One such yearly custom is the family's intricate Thanksgiving festivity. Past the standard banquet, the family has added an unmistakable touch by consolidating an appreciation custom. Every relative pauses for a minute to offer their genuine thanks, pondering the gifts of the previous year. This custom not just adds a significant aspect to the festival yet additionally reinforces the family's bond by encouraging an aggregate appreciation for the lavishness of their lives.

One more valued yearly custom is the family setting up camp excursion throughout the late spring. Which began as an unconstrained escape has developed into an eagerly awaited occasion that unites various ages. From setting up tents to sharing stories around the open air fire, this custom exemplifies the effortlessness of fellowship in nature. It possesses become an energy for the family to detach from the hecticness of regular daily existence and reconnect with one another against the background of nature.

Achievement Festivities:

The family's extraordinary embroidered artwork is additionally decorated with the dynamic tints of achievement festivities. From birthday events to commemorations and graduations, these events become open doors for the family to meet up in euphoric festival. What separates these achievements is the customized and significant manner by which the family decides to celebrate them.

A particular custom for birthday celebrations is the "World of fond memories" custom. Rather than customary presents, every relative contributes a written by hand letter describing affectionate recollections and communicating sincere wishes for the birthday celebrant.

These letters are gathered and introduced as a remembrance, making a mother lode of affection and sentimentality. This custom adds an individual touch to birthday events as well as builds up the obligations of love and shared history inside the family.

Commemorations are commended with a one of a kind turn - a family-made time case. Every year, relatives contribute things, letters, or keepsakes representing huge minutes from the beyond a year. The time container is then fixed, to be opened and returned to on the accompanying commemoration. This custom fills in as a wonderful illustration for the family's excursion, typifying the progression of time and the aggregate development and encounters they've shared.

Graduations are commended with a sincere function directed by the family. Each graduate is embellished with a high quality lei made by relatives, implying the scholarly accomplishment as well as the familial help that has went with the instructive excursion. This custom transforms the graduation function into a profoundly private and genuinely resounding occasion, stressing the significance of family bonds even with achievements.

Social Festivals:

Woven into the family's one of a kind embroidery are strings of social festivals that mirror the different legacy embraced by its individuals. These festivals are an investigation and confirmation of the family's underlying foundations, making a mosaic of customs that mix consistently into the texture of their common personality.

Chinese New Year is a dynamic and treasured social festival inside the family. The celebrations stretch out past the standard red envelopes and winged serpent moves. The family has created their special practices, including a day devoted to narrating about familial legacy. Older folks share stories of family ancestry, underlining the significance of passing down social heritages to more youthful ages. This festival turns into a scaffold among at various times, encouraging a profound appreciation for the family's social legacy.

Diwali, the celebration of lights, is one more social festival that holds unique importance for the family. Past the conventional lights and desserts, the family participates in an aggregate thoughtful gesture during Diwali. Every part takes part locally administration project, typifying the soul of giving and empathy. This interesting custom enhances the family's Diwali festivity as well as supports the upsides of benevolence and social obligation.

Occasional Customs:

The family's embroidered artwork is adorned with the evolving seasons, every one set apart by unmistakable customs that catch the quintessence of that specific season. From the principal blossom of spring to the freshness of harvest time, these occasional customs add a dynamic and repeating beat to the family's aggregate life.

An eagerly awaited custom throughout the colder time of year season is the family's "Celebration of Lights." As the days develop more limited, the family meets up to make handcrafted lamps, each addressing an expectation, a wish, or a goal for the impending year. These lamps are then enlightened during a night gathering, changing the family home into a warm and happy display. This custom lights up the colder time of year evenings as well as fills in as a representative token of aggregate desires.

Springtime rejuvenates the family's cultivating custom. What started as a straightforward establishing action has developed into a collective exertion that includes watching out for a common nursery. Every relative adds to the development of blossoms, spices, and vegetables. This occasional practice yields an abundance of new produce as well as turns into a similitude for the family's obligation to development, supporting, and the recurrent idea of life.

Shared Culinary Traditions:

No exhibit of family customs would be finished without a brief look into the family's common culinary traditions. The kitchen turns into a hallowed space where ages meet up to make and relish dishes that convey the kinds of custom and the glow of shared recollections.

Sunday early lunch has turned into a dearest culinary practice inside the family. The menu is a diverse blend of family top picks, from grandmother's flapjacks to father's omelets. What separates this custom is the cooperative exertion - every relative contributes a dish, transforming the feast into a potluck of affection and flavors. Sunday informal breakfast turns into a period for chuckling, association, and the joy of fellowshipping together.

The family's yearly "Iron Gourmet expert" rivalry is a culinary event that rises above the customary family dinner. Every part chooses a mysterious fixing, and the test is to make a dish that features that fixing. This accommodating contest exhibits the family's culinary innovativeness as well as transforms the kitchen into a space for cordial contention and shared delight.

Generational Traditions:

The family's extraordinary embroidered artwork is unpredictably woven with generational traditions that mirror the passing down of shrewdness, values, and familial associations. These traditions make an extension between the encounters of the more established age and the yearnings of the more youthful, encouraging a feeling of coherence and shared inheritance.

One such generational custom is the family narrating night. Elderly folks amuse more youthful individuals with stories of the family's ancestry, conferring life illustrations, and sharing tales that range across time. This custom not just jam the oral history of the family yet in addition cultivates a more profound comprehension of the aggregate excursion that ties ages together.

Another generational custom is the creating of a family quilt. Every relative contributes a square, embellished with images, pictures, or words that address their uniqueness. As the blanket develops throughout the long term, it turns into an unmistakable portrayal of the family's advancing story. This generational custom transforms a basic material into a loved relic, interfacing relatives across existence.

In the grandstand of the family's novel customs and festivities, an embroidery of affection, association, and shared encounters spreads out. From yearly ceremonies to achievement festivities, social celebrations, and generational traditions, each string winds around together to make a rich story that characterizes the family's personality.

These customs are not simple schedules; they are living articulations of the family's qualities, desires, and aggregate soul. They act as tokens of the significance of association, the magnificence of variety, and the strength that comes from respecting the past while embracing the present.

As the family keeps on adding new join to its embroidery, the exhibit of customs turns into a dynamic and developing articulation of their common process. It is a festival of solidarity, a demonstration of flexibility, and an impression of the persevering through bonds that change a family into a no nonsense embroidery of affection and association.

5.2 Highlighting the joy that comes from shared festivities.

The delight radiating from shared merriments is a dynamic embroidery woven with strings of giggling, association, and a feeling of public festival. In this investigation, we dig into the complex idea of happiness during shared merriments, disentangling the layers that make these minutes so significantly enhancing. From the wizardry of aggregate cheer to the bonds manufactured through shared encounters, the festival of bliss turns into a bringing together power that rises above individual satisfaction and makes an embroidery of shared recollections.

The Wizardry of Aggregate Cheerfulness:

One of the captivating parts of shared celebrations is the enchantment of aggregate joy. Whether it's a family assembling, a local area occasion, or a social festival, the air becomes mixed with a discernible energy that stems from the common delight of those partaking. The giggling, music, and shared articulations of enjoyment make an environment where individual delights mix into an aggregate orchestra of bliss.

Consider a merry Christmas season where loved ones meet up to celebrate. The common expectation, the trading of sincere good tidings, and the aggregate savor the experience of bubbly adornments make a vibe that goes past individual joy. A public foam lifts the soul, transforming standard minutes into phenomenal recollections.

This enchantment isn't bound to great festivals yet reaches out to the basic delights of shared ceremonies. Consider a gathering of companions gathering for a week by week game evening or a local area meeting up for a local grill. The common happiness at these times resembles an attractive power, moving individuals nearer and cultivating a feeling of association that rises above the quick celebrations.

Association and Fellowship:

At the core of shared celebrations is the significant feeling of association and fellowship. Whether it's a social celebration, a strict festival, or an individual achievement, the demonstration of meeting up intensifies the delight experienced by every person. The common space turns into a vessel for making bonds, cultivating understanding, and supporting the feeling of having a place.

Consider a social festival that unites individuals from different foundations. The common merriments become a scaffold, permitting people to interface over normal practices, food, and customs. It's in this common experience that the delight rises above individual limits, making an embroidery of solidarity and shared personality.

Family social events, particularly during occasions, epitomize the profundity of association and fellowship that common celebrations bring. The delight of rejoining with friends and family, the glow of shared feasts, and the aggregate memory of treasured recollections make a familial embroidery where the strings of adoration and harmony are firmly woven.

Making Enduring Recollections:

The delight got from shared merriments reaches out past the vaporous snapshots of festivity; it engraves itself on the material of memory, making enduring impressions that persevere over the long run. Shared encounters during celebrations become the shades that variety the recollections, transforming them into dynamic previews that people convey with them long after the merriments have closed.

Consider a wedding festivity where loved ones accumulate to observe and take part in the blissful association of two people. The common chuckling, the dance floor loaded up with extravagant moves, and the aggregate kindly words become fundamental pieces of the couple's common history. These minutes, woven into the texture of the festival, become loved recollections that several conveys into their excursion together.

Likewise, social merriments frequently include customs and ceremonies that have been gone down through ages. Every festival turns into a connection in the chain of shared legacy, with the delight experienced by one age improving the aggregate memory of the whole local area. These enduring recollections become a wellspring of social personality, interfacing people to their underlying foundations and encouraging a feeling of congruity.

Cultivating a Feeling of Having a place:

The delight intrinsic in shared merriments assumes a vital part in cultivating a significant feeling of having a place. Whether it's celebrating strict occasions, comprehensive developments, or individual accomplishments, the demonstration of meeting up in happy events builds up the possibility that people are essential for an option that could be bigger than themselves. It's a festival of shared values, shared encounters, and shared character that weaves people into the texture of a bigger local area.

Consider a strict festival where individuals from a local area meet up to celebrate a huge occasion. The common supplications, customs, and articulations of confidence make an aggregate feeling of having a place that goes past individual otherworldliness. It's in these common snapshots of bliss and worship that people feel associated with a bigger profound family, tracking down comfort and strength in the common experience.

Local area occasions, like celebrations or fairs, embody how shared merriments add to a feeling of having a place. The delight of taking part in aggregate exercises, participating in public practices, and collaborating with neighbors makes a bond that rises above the individualistic parts of current life. It's a festival of local area soul, where the delight of one turns into the delight of all.

Enhancing Positive Feelings:

Shared merriments have a wonderful capacity to intensify positive feelings, making a far reaching influence that pervades the shared awareness. Whether it's the excitement of a games triumph, the celebration of a fruitful local area project, or the happiness of individual accomplishments, the common euphoria duplicates the positive feelings experienced by every person.

Consider the rapture of a local area meeting up to commend a fruitful magnanimous drive. The common delight of having a beneficial outcome on the existences of others intensifies the singular fulfillment of patrons as well as makes a feeling of shared achievement. It's at these times of aggregate euphoria that the soul of philanthropy and local area administration is reinforced.

Essentially, the delight of shared accomplishments inside a family, like a graduation, advancement, or achievement birthday, is amplified when celebrated all in all. The help, support, and shared pride make a profound reverberation that improves the singular experience. It's undeniably true's that common merriments celebrate achievements as well as extend the close to home associations inside the nuclear family.

Social Trade and Understanding:

Shared celebrations act as a strong stage for social trade and understanding. At the point when people from various foundations meet up to commend each other's practices, a wonderful embroidery of variety unfurls. The delight experienced at these times turns into an impetus for separating social hindrances, cultivating sympathy, and advancing a more profound comprehension of each other.

Consider a multicultural celebration where networks from different foundations merge to commend their interesting customs. The common delight in encountering different music, dance, and cooking styles turns into an extension that rises above social contrasts. It's in these common snapshots of festivity that people gain a more profound appreciation for the lavishness of human variety, developing a feeling of receptiveness and inclusivity.

Family festivities that consolidate components from various social foundations likewise add to social trade inside a microcosm. The delight of mixing customs, sharing stories, and finding out about one another's traditions turns into a festival of the family's variety. It's a demonstration of the possibility that, in common merriments, social contrasts are endured as well as celebrated and embraced.

Developing a Positive Air:

The delight experienced in shared merriments groundbreakingly affects the environment in which these festivals unfurl. Whether it's a work environment occasion, a local area meeting, or a family get-together, the aggregate happiness makes a positive and inspiring vibe that encourages a feeling of fellowship and shared help.

Consider a work environment festivity to stamp a huge accomplishment or achievement. The common delight of achieving a shared objective lifts the general mood as well as establishes a positive workplace. It's at these times of shared achievement and festivity that partners manufacture more grounded bonds, adding to a cooperative and spurred work environment culture.

Family gatherings, set apart by shared chuckling, shared stories, and shared feasts, make a positive environment that reinforces familial bonds. The upbeat communications during these get-togethers add to a feeling of solidarity and shared help. It's a festival of the family's strength, aggregate achievements, and the getting through associations that endure everyday hardship.

Empowering Thoughtful gestures:

The delight experienced during shared merriments frequently stretches out past the quick festival, empowering thoughtful gestures and liberality. Whether it's through magnanimous drives during local area occasions, acts of kindness inside a family, or articulations of generosity among companions, the common bliss turns into an impetus for spreading energy and having an effect in the existences of others.

Consider a birthday festivity where, rather than conventional presents, the individual urges loved ones to add to a worthy mission. The common delight of offering back turns into a fundamental piece of the festival, changing the demonstration of getting into a valuable chance to have a beneficial outcome on the local area. It's a festival of liberality, empathy, and the delight that comes from adding to the prosperity of others.

Likewise, people group occasions that consolidate components of social obligation, like pledge drives or volunteer drives, become festivities of aggregate generosity. The common satisfaction in making a positive commitment to society fortifies the securities inside the local area and cultivates a feeling of shared liability. A festival goes past individual satisfaction, embracing that bliss is increased when it is shared to help others.

5.3 Illustration of how small gatherings can create meaningful connections.

The private material of little social events paints a nuanced picture of significant associations, where the nuance of shared minutes makes an embroidery of warmth, understanding, and certifiable human cooperation. In this investigation, we dive into the complexities of how these unassuming congregations, be they family suppers, companion social events, or relaxed meet-ups, have the groundbreaking ability to produce associations that run profound. It is inside the folds of these little social occasions that the magnificence of genuineness, shared weakness, and the enchantment of human association show some signs of life.

Genuineness in Cozy Spaces:

Little social events give a material where validness becomes the overwhelming focus. Not at all like bigger occasions where social elements might incline towards execution, more modest settings offer the solace for people to act naturally. Whether it's a family supper, a book club meeting, or a tranquil espresso find companions, the closeness of the space permits individuals to let down their gatekeeper, encouraging real associations.

Consider a supper gathering among companions where the setting is a close lawn. The climate is loose, the lighting is delicate, and the discussion streams normally. Here, people go ahead and offer their viewpoints, share individual stories, and participate in discussions that go past the surface. The realness that flourishes in these little get-togethers turns into the establishment for significant associations.

Family suppers, specifically, represent the force of legitimacy in personal spaces. The commonality of countenances, shared history, and the solace of a home setting establish a climate where relatives can be their actual selves. It's inside these affectionate social affairs that ages share chuckling, stories, and, surprisingly, calm minutes, extending the bonds that integrate them.

Shared Weakness:

Little social events offer an asylum for shared weakness, where people have a good sense of security enough to open up, express their sentiments, and interface on a more significant level. The closeness of these settings considers the affirmation of shared battles, desires, and feelings, making a space where weakness turns into an extension to significant associations.

Consider a care group meeting where people confronting comparable difficulties meet up in a little, confiding in setting. The common weakness inside this space turns into a strong impetus for association. As people express their feelings of dread, expectations, and encounters, a feeling of sympathy and understanding penetrates the gathering, making securities that stretch out past the span of the gathering.

Essentially, affectionate companion social affairs frequently include snapshots of shared weakness. Whether it's examining individual difficulties, looking for exhortation, or communicating frailties, the private setting permits companions to show up for one another in significant ways. It's inside these little circles that people track down comfort, understanding, and a feeling of association that goes past the outer layer of easygoing connections.

The Enchantment of Significant Discussions:

In the domain of little social affairs, significant discussions unfurl like sensitive blooms, each word adding to the lavishness of association. The predetermined number of members in these settings considers further and more engaged exchanges, making a space where people can genuinely draw in with each other.

Consider a little book club meeting where individuals assemble to examine a book. The engaged idea of the get-together cultivates a climate where scholarly investigation flawlessly changes into individual reflections. At these times, significant discussions rise above the limits of the book, giving way to conversations about existence, esteems, and shared encounters.

Family get-togethers, where the quantity of members is reasonable, likewise give a phase to significant discussions. Whether it's finding a cousin, sharing life refreshes with an auntie, or taking part in sincere discussions with grandparents, the personal setting considers the trading of stories, shrewdness, and points of view. These discussions become strings in the familial embroidery, winding around a story that rises above time.

Making Enduring Recollections:

The closeness of little social affairs adds to the production of enduring recollections, scratched with the extravagance of shared encounters. Not at all like bigger occasions that might obscure into a montage of countenances and exercises, the uniqueness of these more modest settings guarantees that every second is loved and recollected.

Consider a comfortable evening gathering where companions accumulate around a table decorated with custom made dishes. The giggling, the ringing of glasses, and the common delight in food make a climate where everything about engraved in the aggregate memory. These little minutes become piece of the common history of the gathering, making recollections that persevere past the actual occasion.

Family get-aways, where the prompt circle is available, represent the production of enduring recollections inside little social occasions. Whether it's a basic ocean side day or an end of the week escape, the common encounters become standards in the family's story. The photos, within jokes, and the aggregate memory of these minutes structure an embroidery of shared recollections that reinforce familial bonds.

Encouraging Further Comprehension:

In the closeness of little social events, a more profound comprehension of each other unfurls. The subtleties of individual characters, the complexities of individual stories, and the nuances of shared values become more obvious in these affectionate settings. It is inside this understanding that genuine associations track down their underlying foundations.

Consider an independent venture meeting where colleagues assemble to examine a task. The nearby coordinated effort in this close setting considers a nuanced comprehension of each colleague's assets, difficulties, and commitments. It is inside this common perspective that compelling cooperation is encouraged, laying the basis for a fruitful coordinated effort.

In family settings, especially during little social occasions, the subtleties of individual connections become more articulated. The elements between kin, the interesting connection among parent and youngster, and the exchange of characters add to a more profound comprehension of relational peculiarities. It's inside these close minutes that familial associations are fortified, and a significant comprehension of each other is sustained.

Developing Trust and Association:

Trust is the bedrock whereupon significant associations flourish, and little social affairs give the rich ground to its development. The closeness of these settings permits people to construct trust naturally, making an establishment for valid associations with prosper.

In a treatment bunch, where people meet up to share individual battles, the little, steady setting encourages a climate of trust. As members focus on their encounters, fears, and expectations, a feeling of shared trust creates. It is inside this believing space that people feel appreciated, comprehended, and associated with other people who are exploring comparative excursions.

Essentially, inside the structure of dear fellowships, trust is developed through shared encounters in little social occasions. The weakness to act naturally, the affirmation of privacy, and the common history add to the structure of trust. It's inside these circles of trust that fellowships develop, and the associations between people become tough.

The Magnificence of Implicit Associations:

Little social affairs frequently lead to the excellence of implicit associations - those quiet trades, shared looks, and silent signals that convey understanding and association without the requirement for unequivocal articulation. In the nuance of these implicit associations, a significant language of shared feeling arises.

Consider a family supper where a look between kin imparts a common memory or an inside joke. The implicit association at that time exemplifies long periods of shared encounters, making a bond that rises above the requirement for verbal enunciation. It is inside these nonverbal trades that the quintessence of familial association is refined.

Companion get-togethers, as well, are ready with implicit associations. Whether it's a common grin across the room or a realizing look traded during a discussion, these implicit minutes embody the profundity of understanding between companions. It's in these silent trades that fellowships are reaffirmed, and the connections between people are hardened.

The Effect on Private Prosperity:

The meaning of little get-togethers stretches out past the domain of social associations; it significantly affects individual prosperity. The closeness of these settings gives a feeling of having a place, daily encouragement, and the certification of one's worth inside a local area.

Consider a care group for people confronting comparable difficulties, for example, a distress support bunch. The little and close nature of the social event takes into consideration shared encounters, common comprehension, and a feeling of brotherhood. It is inside this strong space that people track down comfort, solace, and the approval of their feelings, adding to their profound prosperity.

Family get-togethers, particularly during significant life altering situations or achievements, add to a feeling of having a place and prosperity. Whether it's commending accomplishments, offering profound help during difficulties, or essentially partaking in the organization of friends and family, the little and close nature of these social events encourages a profound feeling of association. It is inside the hug of family that people track down strength, love, and a feeling of prosperity.

Chapter 6

"Challenges and Solidarity"

In the complicated dance of human life, challenges arise as the stone carvers of strength and fortitude, molding the forms of our aggregate process. This investigation digs into the diverse connection among difficulties and fortitude, disentangling the strings that wind around together the common encounters, shared battles, and shared wins that characterize the human story. From individual misfortunes to worldwide emergencies, the transaction among difficulties and fortitude uncovers the wonderful limit of people and networks to join despite difficulty, making an embroidery that rises above the limits of situation.

Individual Difficulties:

At the core of the human experience lie individual difficulties — the singular battles and difficulties that shape our way of living. Whether it's confronting well-being emergencies, exploring vocation difficulties, or managing individual misfortune, these difficulties become pots for flexibility and, startlingly, for the fortitude that arises because of shared battles.

Consider an individual doing combating a persistent sickness. The everyday difficulties, physical and close to home cost, and the vulnerabilities that go with such an excursion are significant.

However, inside this individual difficulty, an exceptional type of fortitude frequently emerges — an organization of help that might incorporate companions, family, and even colleagues who rally together to give support, understanding, and a common strength that facilitates the weight of the person.

Essentially, in the domain of emotional well-being difficulties, the fortitude that rises up out of shared battles has the ability to break shame and encourage a feeling of local area. As people focus on their encounters with emotional well-being, an aggregate comprehension creates, making a space where shared weaknesses become strings that tight spot individuals together. Support gatherings, online networks, and promotion endeavors come out from the fortitude conceived out of the common excursion of conquering emotional well-being difficulties.

Local area Strength in Catastrophic events:

On a more extensive scale, challenges reach out past individual encounters to envelop aggregate preliminaries looked by networks. Catastrophic events, with their overwhelming effect on lives and foundation, uncover the profundity of local area strength and the fortitude that arises in the fallout of disaster.

Consider a local area wrestling with the fallout of a typhoon. The obliteration, uprooting, and the difficult course of revamping become shared difficulties that tight spot local area individuals together. In these difficult times, the natural human impulse for fortitude comes to the front as people team up in salvage endeavors, give sanctuary to those out of luck, and add to the aggregate recuperation. The difficulties become a pot for local area fortitude, building up the interconnectedness of mankind notwithstanding difficulty.

Worldwide occasions, like the Coronavirus pandemic, embody the interconnected idea of difficulties and the worldwide fortitude that can arise accordingly. The common danger of a far and wide infection incited aggregate activity on an uncommon scale. Countries teamed up in logical exploration, people complied to general well-being rules for everyone's benefit, and networks upheld each other through shared help drives. The pandemic, while an imposing test, turned into an impetus for worldwide fortitude, stressing the significance of aggregate liability and interconnectedness in exploring shared misfortunes.

Fortitude in Friendly Developments:

Challenges frequently manifest as foundational treacheries that saturate social orders, bringing about friendly developments that try to address and redress these issues. The social liberties development, women's activist developments, and other support endeavors highlight the groundbreaking force of fortitude chasing equity and balance.

Think about the social liberties development in the US during the mid-twentieth hundred years. The difficulties presented by racial isolation, separation, and fundamental disparity electrifies people from assorted foundations to stand together in fortitude.

Through serene fights, demonstrations of common defiance, and the force of aggregate voices, the development achieved critical administrative and cultural changes. The fortitude produced despite foundational challenges turned into a main thrust for civil rights.

Women's activist developments overall correspondingly epitomize the strength of fortitude in tending to orientation based difficulties. From supporting for ladies' testimonial to battling against orientation based brutality, these developments have united people across ages, foundations, and societies. The common obligation to destroying man centric designs and accomplishing orientation fairness turns into a bringing together power that rises above individual encounters, making a worldwide embroidery of fortitude despite orientation based difficulties.

Worldwide Difficulties and Global Fortitude:

In the 21st hundred years, worldwide difficulties have become the overwhelming focus, stressing the interconnectedness of the world and the basic for global fortitude. Issues, for example, environmental change, neediness, and general wellbeing emergencies require cooperative endeavors on a worldwide scale to impact significant change.

Consider the test of environmental change, which knows no boundaries and influences networks all over the planet. The common danger to the planet's biological systems has incited worldwide participation, as countries meet up to arrange arrangements, set emanation decrease targets, and execute feasible practices. The worldwide test turns into a source of inspiration for global fortitude, underlining the common obligation of all countries in protecting the planet for people in the future.

General wellbeing challenges, as featured by the reaction to pandemics like Coronavirus, additionally highlight the significance of worldwide fortitude. The interconnectedness of movement and exchange implies that a wellbeing emergency one region of the planet can immediately turn into a worldwide test. Worldwide cooperation in immunization improvement, dissemination of clinical assets, and composed general wellbeing measures mirrors the aggregate reaction to a common worldwide danger.

Difficulties and Fortitude in Instructive Strengthening:

Instruction, while a useful asset for strengthening, frequently faces difficulties that require aggregate endeavors to survive. Variations in admittance to quality schooling, boundaries looked by underestimated networks, and fundamental issues inside schooling systems are among the difficulties that fuel developments for instructive strengthening and fortitude.

Consider the difficulties looked by networks where admittance to instruction is restricted, especially for young ladies. The worldwide development for young ladies' schooling, exemplified by drives like Malala Asset, underlines the extraordinary force of fortitude.

People, associations, and countries join in the common conviction that training is a key right, and aggregate endeavors are directed into separating boundaries, supporting for strategy changes, and setting out open doors for instructive strengthening.

Additionally, challenges inside schooling systems, like imbalances in assets and amazing open doors, brief developments for instructive change. The fortitude among teachers, understudies, and networks upholding for a more comprehensive and impartial schooling system turns into a main impetus for change. The common vision of schooling as a pathway to strengthening cultivates joint effort in tending to fundamental difficulties and pursuing an all the more and open instructive scene.

Challenges as Impetuses for Development and Progress:

In the many-sided exchange of difficulties and fortitude, difficulty frequently fills in as an impetus for development and progress. When confronted with shared difficulties, people and networks join as they continued looking for arrangements, igniting inventiveness, strength, and an aggregate assurance to defeat impediments.

Consider the difficulties presented by mechanical disturbance in the gig market. The appearance of mechanization and man-made reasoning has raised worries about work dislodging and the requirement for reskilling the labor force. Because of these difficulties, fortitude arises as instructive drives, preparing programs, and cooperative endeavors among ventures and states. The common objective of adjusting to mechanical changes turns into a main thrust for advancement, at last prompting the improvement of new abilities, ventures, and financial open doors.

General wellbeing challenges, like the rise of new irresistible sicknesses, also spike cooperative endeavors and inventive arrangements. The worldwide reaction to the HIV/Helps pestilence, for instance, united researchers, medical services experts, activists, and legislatures in a common mission to grasp, treat, and forestall the spread of the infection. The difficulties presented by the scourge turned into an impetus for headways in clinical exploration, medical services conveyance, and worldwide participation in tending to irresistible illnesses.

Fortitude Even with Existential Dangers:

Existential dangers, whether regular or human-made, have the one of a kind capacity to rise above individual and aggregate contrasts, provoking an instinctual call for fortitude despite shared hazard. From worldwide dangers of atomic struggle to the possible outcomes of ecological breakdown, the acknowledgment of shared weakness encourages an aggregate reaction that rises above boundaries and philosophies.

Consider the existential danger presented by atomic weapons during the Virus War. The common acknowledgment of the disastrous outcomes of atomic clash prompted worldwide endeavors to forestall the utilization of such weapons.

Settlements, demilitarization discussions, and grassroots developments pushing for atomic restraint became articulations of worldwide fortitude chasing after harmony and endurance.

Likewise, the approaching ghost of natural breakdown, driven by environmental change and biological debasement, has incited a worldwide development for ecological maintainability. The mutual perspective that the soundness of the planet is complicatedly connected to the prosperity of every one of its occupants has prompted aggregate endeavors to address natural difficulties. Peaceful accords, preservation drives, and grassroots developments for natural equity mirror the fortitude that arises even with an existential danger to the planet.

Challenges as Impetuses for Social Union:

In the cauldron of difficulties, social union arises as a strong power that ties networks together. The common experience of confronting misfortune encourages a feeling of having a place, compassion, and shared help that rises above individual contrasts, making a versatile social texture.

Consider a local area wrestling with monetary difficulties, like employment misfortune or monetary precariousness. Despite these common battles, social union turns into a wellspring of solidarity. Common guide organizations, local area drives to give assets, and the aggregate work to help weak individuals epitomize the fortitude that emerges in the midst of financial difficulty. The difficulties become an impetus for social union, building up the interconnectedness of local area individuals.

Additionally, social union appears in light of difficulties connected with social personality and variety. In multicultural social orders, the difficulties of exploring social contrasts and battling segregation brief developments for inclusivity and correspondence. The common obligation to encouraging a different and open minded society turns into a bringing together power that rises above individual foundations, adding to social union.

Defeating Difficulties Through Interconnectedness:

The interconnectedness of difficulties and fortitude features the cooperative connection among individual and aggregate prosperity. As people explore individual misfortunes, networks wrestle with foundational treacheries, and the world stands up to worldwide dangers, the acknowledgment of shared battles cultivates a feeling of interconnectedness that rises above individual interests.

Consider the idea of ubuntu, an African way of thinking underscoring the interconnectedness of mankind. The adage "I'm since we are" epitomizes the substance of fortitude in beating difficulties. It perceives that singular prosperity is indivisible from the prosperity of the local area and the bigger world. In embracing this interconnectedness, people and networks track down strength in solidarity and versatility in common perspective.

In the domain of general wellbeing, the interconnectedness of difficulties and fortitude is apparent in the idea of group resistance. The aggregate work to inoculate a populace against irresistible infections features the common obligation to safeguard weak people and forestall the spread of sickness. The difficulties presented by infection become a source of inspiration for aggregate prosperity through inoculation and general wellbeing measures.

Difficulties, Fortitude, and the Human Soul:

At the center of the connection among difficulties and fortitude lies the unyielding soul of humankind. The capacity to join despite difficulty, to relate to the battles of others, and to work all in all towards shared objectives is a demonstration of the flexibility and strength intrinsic in the human soul.

Consider the accounts of people who have confronted exceptional difficulties, from overcomers of catastrophic events to activists battling for civil rights. The consistent idea in these accounts is the human soul's ability to transcend difficulty through thoughtful gestures, fortitude, and a common obligation to making a superior future. The difficulties become a cauldron that uncovers the phenomenal expected inside the human soul for fortitude and aggregate activity.

In the midst of emergency, articulations of fortitude frequently appear as regular courage — the sacrificial demonstrations of people who broaden some assistance, offer help to those out of luck, and exhibit the groundbreaking force of sympathy. These demonstrations, whether on an individual or worldwide scale, typify the strength of the human soul even with difficulties.

6.1 Discussion of challenges faced by the family.

The family, as the crucial unit of society, is a microcosm of human connections where difficulties are innate to its dynamic nature. Inside the private limits of familial bonds, people explore a perplexing landscape that envelops different characters, contrasting necessities, and the inescapable contentions that emerge from shared lives. This investigation digs into the complex difficulties looked by families, including relational elements, outside pressures, and the flexibility expected to endure the hardships that test the texture of familial connections.

Relational Elements:

At the core of everyday life are the many-sided relational elements that characterize connections between guardians, kin, and more distant family individuals. These elements, while rich with affection and association, additionally bring about difficulties established in the variety of individual characters, correspondence styles, and contrasting assumptions.

Think about the difficulties inside parent-youngster connections, where the developing requirements of developing kids might conflict with the assumptions and nurturing styles of guardians. The fragile harmony between sustaining freedom and giving direction requires progressing discussion, and misalignment in these elements can prompt struggles.

The test lies in cultivating a climate that supports open correspondence, common comprehension, and the adaptability to adjust as the two guardians and youngsters explore the intricacies of self-improvement.

Kin elements, set apart by shared history and special bonds, additionally present difficulties as people with particular characters coincide inside the nuclear family. Kin contention, rivalry for parental consideration, and the unavoidable struggles that emerge according to varying points of view are normal difficulties. Arranging these elements requires developing a feeling of decency, advancing sympathy among kin, and encouraging a climate where clashes become open doors for development and understanding.

More distant family elements further add to the intricacy of relational connections inside the nuclear family. Contrasting qualities, generational holes, and fluctuating degrees of contribution can prompt difficulties together as one. Finding some kind of harmony among independence and familial associations becomes fundamental, as people explore the many-sided trap of more distant family connections while keeping up with the center securities that characterize the family.

Correspondence Difficulties:

Successful correspondence is the soul of solid connections, and inside the family, challenges in correspondence can lead to false impressions, hatred, and a breakdown in associations. These difficulties might originate from contrasts in correspondence styles, implicit assumptions, or the reluctance to address delicate subjects.

Think about the test of viable parent-youngster correspondence, where the age hole might add to errors. Guardians might battle to get a handle on the subtleties of quickly changing cultural standards, while youngsters might find it trying to communicate their developing viewpoints. Spanning this correspondence hole requires a promise to undivided attention, compassion, and making a space where the two ages feel appreciated and comprehended.

Kin correspondence, as well, faces obstacles as people with particular characters explore shared spaces. Varying correspondence styles, unsettled clashes, and implicit complaints can strain kin connections. Conquering these difficulties includes cultivating a climate where transparent correspondence is supported, and clashes are addressed usefully instead of permitted to putrefy.

More distant family correspondence challenges frequently spin around the sensitive equilibrium of remaining associated without interrupting individual security. Miscommunications can prompt sensations of avoidance, errors, or even strain inside the more distant family organization. Exploring these difficulties requires laying out clear limits, keeping up with open lines of correspondence, and cultivating an environment of shared regard among relatives.

Monetary Tensions:

Monetary difficulties are an omnipresent part of day to day life, influencing all that from day to day living to long haul desires. The need to accommodate essential necessities, plan for the future, and explore unforeseen costs can overwhelm familial connections.

Consider the strain on guardians to give a steady and secure monetary climate for their youngsters. Adjusting the requests of work, overseeing family funds, and guaranteeing an agreeable way of life for the family can prompt pressure and, on occasion, deep-seated insecurities. The test lies in tending to monetary tensions cooperatively, cultivating open correspondence about planning and monetary objectives, and guaranteeing that the quest for financial soundness doesn't eclipse the profound prosperity of the family.

Monetary difficulties can likewise affect kin connections, especially when assets are restricted or when there are differences in monetary help. The potential for desire, hatred, or sensations of disparity might emerge. Alleviating these difficulties includes advancing a comprehension of shared liabilities, empowering monetary proficiency inside the family, and developing a climate where open conversations about cash are standardized.

More distant family elements might additionally muddle monetary difficulties, particularly when relatives have shifting financial conditions. Finding some kind of harmony between supporting each other and regarding individual monetary independence becomes significant. The test lies in exploring these abberations with sympathy, keeping away from judgment, and finding cooperative arrangements that advance the aggregate prosperity of the more distant family.

Life Advances and Change:

Life is set apart by advances, from the cheerful achievements of marriage and the introduction of youngsters to the unavoidable difficulties presented by sickness, misfortune, and the progression of time. Exploring these changes as a family requires versatility, flexibility, and the capacity to help each other through the rhythmic movement of life's excursion.

Consider the difficulties presented by significant life changes, like the appearance of another relative. While the introduction of a kid is a blissful event, it likewise carries critical acclimations to schedules, rest designs, and the elements between accomplices. The test lies in adjusting to these progressions as a unit, sharing liabilities, and encouraging a climate of help as the family extends.

Youthfulness, set apart by the change from adolescence to adulthood, presents interesting difficulties as people wrestle with personality arrangement and the quest for autonomy. Guardians might wind up exploring the sensitive harmony among direction and permitting independence. The test is to cultivate an environment of common regard, open exchange, and backing as relatives explore the groundbreaking excursion of youth.

Sickness and misfortune are impressive difficulties that can test the strength of familial bonds. The profound cost of really focusing on a wiped out relative, the pain experienced despite misfortune, and the changes expected to oblige changes in relational peculiarities request versatility and empathy. Exploring these difficulties includes establishing a strong climate where feelings are recognized, and relatives have a good sense of security communicating their weaknesses.

Social and Between generational Difficulties:

Social and between generational difficulties inside families are in many cases established in varying qualities, convictions, and assumptions. These difficulties might rise up out of the crossing point of assorted social foundations, generational holes, and the developing idea of cultural standards.

Consider families where individuals have a place with various social foundations, each with its own arrangement of customs, customs, and assumptions. The test lies in exploring these social distinctions while cultivating a comprehensive climate that regards and celebrates variety. Correspondence, shared understanding, and a readiness to gain from each other are fundamental in beating social difficulties inside the family.

Generational holes, affected by changing cultural standards and mechanical headways, can prompt false impressions and contrasts in standpoint. The test is for various ages inside the family to connect these holes, figuring out something worth agreeing on while regarding individual points of view. Working with between generational comprehension includes open correspondence, shared encounters, and an acknowledgment of the significant bits of knowledge every age brings to the relational intricacy.

Adjusting Individual Necessities and Aggregate Prosperity:

One of the essential difficulties inside families is finding some kind of harmony between individual necessities, desires, and self-improvement, and the aggregate prosperity of the nuclear family. The strain between chasing after individual objectives and adding to the concordance of the relational peculiarity requires exchange, split the difference, and a common obligation to shared help.

Consider the test looked by guardians in offsetting their singular interests with the requests of being a parent. The craving for individual satisfaction, vocation yearnings, or taking care of oneself can some of the time struggle with the significant investment expected for viable nurturing. The test lies in finding an amicable equilibrium that considers individual development while guaranteeing the prosperity of the family in general.

Essentially, kin connections might confront difficulties when individual objectives and desires veer. The quest for individual interests, vocation ways, or way of life decisions can make pressure in the event that not drew closer with responsiveness and a comprehension of every kin's remarkable excursion. Beating these difficulties includes encouraging a climate where individual contrasts are praised, and support for every kin's goals is a common family esteem.

The interchange between individual necessities and aggregate prosperity stretches out to more distant family elements, where different relatives might have assorted assumptions for the family's direction. Adjusting the longings and desires of individual nuclear families inside the more distant family structure requires open correspondence, adaptability, and a common obligation to keeping up with familial bonds regardless of contrasting ways.

Beating Difficulty Through Strength:

The difficulties looked by families, various and multifaceted as they might be, highlight the significance of flexibility as a directing power. Flexibility inside the family setting includes the capacity to adjust to change, return quickly from misfortune, and develop a common strength that faces the hardships of life.

Notwithstanding relational difficulties, strength appears as the ability to explore clashes helpfully, gain from shared encounters, and arise more grounded as a unit. It includes a guarantee to constant development, both as people and as an aggregate family substance.

Flexibility in correspondence inside the family includes the development of undivided attention, compassionate comprehension, and the readiness to participate in troublesome discussions. It requires a common obligation to cultivating a correspondence style that advances transparency, genuineness, and shared regard.

Confronting monetary tensions as a family requests strength as cooperative critical thinking, monetary proficiency, and a mutual perspective of needs. Beating monetary provokes includes a pledge to shared help, mindful planning, and the capacity to adjust to changing financial conditions.

Flexibility in exploring life advances requires an aggregate affirmation of the certainty of progress, a common obligation to help each other through changes, and the capacity to track down strength notwithstanding vulnerability. It includes seeing life's changes as any open doors for development and variation.

Social and between generational difficulties are met with strength when families effectively try to comprehend and celebrate variety. Versatility includes the ability to gain from each other, adjust to advancing cultural standards, and embrace the lavishness that different social viewpoints bring to the family woven artwork.

Adjusting individual necessities and aggregate prosperity requires strength in arranging splits the difference, keeping up with adaptability, and cultivating a climate where every relative feels esteemed. Flexibility includes perceiving that singular development adds to the general strength of the family and that aggregate prosperity is based on an underpinning of help and understanding.

6.2 Stories of how the small unit rallies together in times of adversity.

In the terrific woven artwork of familial life, the little unit is in many cases tried by the breezes of difficulty, uncovering the genuine strength that exists in the obligations of connection. These accounts epitomize the flexibility, solidarity, and enduring help that arise when families face difficulties, showing the way that the littlest unit can turn into an imposing power in exploring the tempests of life.

The Story of Wellbeing Difficulties:

In the core of a little family, the connection among guardians and their lone youngster confronted a surprising test when the kid was determined to have a constant medical issue. The underlying shock and dread were substantial, yet rather than capitulating to surrender, the family mobilized together. The guardians became resolute backers for their youngster's medical care, enthusiastically investigating therapy choices, talking with clinical experts, and making an encouraging group of people inside the local area.

The little unit changed their home into a safe-haven of affection and understanding. Plans were acclimated to oblige clinical arrangements, and the family embraced a way of life that focused on the youngster's prosperity. The guardians, in their unified front, exemplified strength, offering steadfast consistent encouragement to their kid, who confronted the difficulties of dealing with an ongoing sickness.

Kin, as well, assumed a urgent part in this familial story. Rather than hatred or sensations of disregard, the kin embraced their jobs as partners. They became advocates by their own doing, teaching companions and colleagues about their kin's condition, encouraging a feeling of sympathy inside their friend bunch. The family's reaction to the wellbeing challenge turned into a demonstration of the force of solidarity, love, and shared liability in defeating misfortune.

Exploring Monetary Strife:

In a little family that had endured the tides of monetary highs and lows, the unexpected cutback of an employment turned into an imposing test. The underlying shockwaves of monetary vulnerability undulated through the family, however the family wouldn't be incapacitated by dread. All things being equal, they clustered together to plan, financial plan, and track down intelligent fixes to explore the tempest.

The guardians, confronted with the possibility of joblessness, went to their abilities and interests. What arose was a little privately-owned company brought about for a specific need and energized by the aggregate gifts inside the unit. The kids, rather than being safeguarded from the monetary difficulties, became dynamic members in the family's pioneering venture, acquiring significant fundamental abilities en route.

The versatility of this little unit was apparent not simply in that frame of mind to adjust to new monetary real factors yet additionally in their steady help for each other. As opposed to permitting monetary tensions to make divisions, the family tracked down strength in their common perspective. The experience, while without a doubt testing, turned into a section in their story that displayed the force of joint effort, imagination, and familial solidarity despite monetary difficulty.

The Story of Misfortune and Sorrow:

In the tranquil corners of a little family, the unexpected loss of a cherished relative cast a shadow over their lives. The melancholy was significant, taking steps to unwind the very texture that kept them intact. However, amidst distress, the little unit revitalized in an aggregate hug of help and comfort.

The lamenting system turned into a common excursion. Instead of withdrawing into individual sadness, the family made spaces for recognition, regarding the recollections of their lost adored one. Customs, customs, and open discussions about their misery became vital pieces of their recuperating interaction.

The strength of the little unit lay in their capacity to hold space for one another's agony. They explored the intricacies of anguish with compassion, understanding that every relative adapted in an unexpected way. The guardians became mainstays of solidarity, giving an establishment to their kids to straightforwardly communicate their feelings. Kin rested on one another for help, producing a significantly more profound bond despite misfortune.

As time elapsed, the family's aggregate flexibility became obvious in their obligation to reconstructing their lives while esteeming the recollections of the left. The experience, however set apart by trouble, turned into a demonstration of the getting through force of familial bonds and the limit of the little unit to endure the hardship of melancholy together.

The Excursion of Instructive Difficulties:

In the domain of schooling, a little family confronted the difficulties of supporting a kid with learning contrasts. Rather than survey it as an obstacle, the family embraced the chance for development and understanding. They energized together to explore the school system, upholding for their youngster's special necessities and guaranteeing that the learning climate was helpful for their prosperity.

Guardians became wild promoters, working together with teachers, looking for particular help, and effectively partaking in their kid's instructive excursion. Kin, as opposed to survey their kin's learning distinctions as an obstruction, became partners chasing scholarly achievement. The family established a sustaining home climate that commended every kid's remarkable assets and commitments.

The little unit's versatility was obvious not simply in the scholarly accomplishments of the youngster with learning contrasts yet in addition in the sympathy and inclusivity encouraged inside the family. The experience turned into a common victory, showing the way that instructive difficulties could be changed into potential open doors for development, understanding, and the reinforcing of familial bonds.

Beating Relational Battles:

Inside the bounds of a little family, relational contentions definitely emerged. The test was not in that frame of mind of conflicts but rather in how the family decided to explore and determine them. As opposed to permitting clashes to rot, the family resolved to open correspondence, undivided attention, and an aggregate work to comprehend each other.

Guardians became good examples for compromise, showing the significance of sound correspondence and split the difference. Kin, rather than survey conflicts as troublesome, took in the specialty of exchange and split the difference inside the nuclear family. The family laid out a culture of profound wellbeing, where every part felt appreciated, esteemed, and upheld.

The little unit's flexibility was obvious in the goal of struggles as well as in the fortified bonds that arose out of these encounters. The capacity to explore relational battles turned into a demonstration of the family's obligation to development, understanding, and the persevering through strength of their associations.

6.3 Reflection on the strength that emerges from facing difficulties as a united front.

In the pot of life's difficulties, families frequently find a repository of solidarity that lies in their capacity to confront troubles as a unified front. This reflection dives into the significant examples gained from the cauldron of difficulty, investigating how the common experience of defeating difficulties fortifies familial bonds, encourages flexibility, and makes an embroidery of solidarity that rises above individual battles.

The Embroidered artwork of Shared Affliction:

Misfortune, in its bunch structures, winds around a consistent idea through the texture of familial life. Whether it be wellbeing challenges, monetary mishaps, misfortune, or relational battles, families wind up exploring a scene set apart by unanticipated hardships. Notwithstanding, inside this embroidery of shared misfortune arises an exceptional strength that ties relatives together.

The common experience of confronting challenges develops sympathy and grasping inside the nuclear family. As every part wrestles with their own difficulties, a shared mindset creates — a common consciousness of the delicacy and strength intrinsic in the human experience. This common perspective turns into the establishment whereupon the family develops its fortitude, perceiving that, even with misfortune, they are in good company however are important for a unified front.

The Pot of Strength:

Difficulty goes about as a pot for flexibility, and families, when stood up to with challenges, have the chance to fashion versatility as an aggregate power. The capacity to return quickly from mishaps, adjust to new conditions, and find strength despite misfortune turns into a common excursion. It is in the cauldron of flexibility that the solidarity of the family is tried and fortified.

Consider a family confronting monetary difficulty. Instead of capitulating to surrender, the aggregate versatility of the family turns into a main thrust for change. Every part contributes their assets, thoughts, and backing, changing the experience of monetary battle into a chance for aggregate development. The family's capacity to adjust and continue on, regardless of the difficulties, exhibits the groundbreaking force of strength when looked as a unified front.

In the pot of versatility, families discover that the aggregate strength got from confronting troubles together is more noteworthy than the amount of individual qualities. It is an update that, in solidarity, they have the strength to endure the hardships and arise more grounded on the opposite side.

Developing Solidarity Through Correspondence:

Correspondence turns into a foundation in the development of familial solidarity in the midst of misfortune. The capacity to transparently share considerations, sentiments, and concerns establishes a steady climate where every relative feels appreciated and comprehended. Compelling correspondence goes about as a scaffold, associating the profound scenes of people and encouraging a feeling of solidarity in exploring difficulties.

During seasons of difficulty, family gatherings, conversations, and, surprisingly, shared reflections become essential in keeping up with open lines of correspondence. These purposeful minutes give a stage to communicating fears, expectations, and yearnings. They make a space where difficulties are recognized by and large, and procedures for beating them are cooperatively contrived.

Even with wellbeing challenges, for example, a family's capacity to convey straightforwardly about the effect of the disease, share their feelings, and on the whole settle on the best strategy reinforces their solidarity. The common perspective that every part's viewpoint is esteemed encourages a culture of help and fortitude.

Correspondence likewise assumes a crucial part in settling clashes that might emerge during testing times. Rather than permitting errors to putrefy, families who impart really address clashes head-on, looking for goals that reinforce instead of crack their bonds. It is through this obligation to transparent correspondence that familial solidarity turns into a versatile power despite misfortune.

The Obligation of Shared Liabilities:

Difficulty frequently requires a reallocation of obligations inside the family. Whether it's really focusing on a debilitated relative, overseeing monetary strains, or exploring life changes, shared liabilities become the paste that ties relatives together. In bearing these obligations on the whole, the family produces a bond that rises above individual jobs and reinforces their feeling of solidarity.

Consider a family really focusing on an older part confronting wellbeing challenges. The common obligation of providing care turns into a binding together power as relatives team up in giving physical, profound, and reasonable help. The experience extends their associations as well as makes a feeling of mutual perspective and obligation to the prosperity of their cherished one.

Likewise, the circulation of obligations during monetary challenges requires an aggregate exertion. Every relative contributes in their own specific manner, whether it's investigating new pay open doors, cutting costs, or offering profound help. The common obligation of exploring monetary difficulties turns into an aggregate undertaking, supporting the idea that the family is a unified front in conquering misfortune.

The bond fashioned through shared liabilities isn't simply a reasonable reaction to challenges; it is an emblematic certification of the family's obligation to each other. That's what it conveys, in the midst of trouble, every part will contribute their endeavors and assets for a long term benefit — a demonstration of the strength that arises while confronting liabilities as a unified front.

Emergency as Impetus for Development:

Difficulty, when confronted on the whole, has the extraordinary ability to catalyze individual and familial development. The difficulties become impetuses for self-revelation, flexibility, and the reinforcing of familial bonds. It is in the cauldron of emergency that families frequently track down undiscovered supplies of solidarity and potential.

Consider a family exploring the intricacies of a youngster's learning distinctions. The common obligation to supporting the youngster's instructive excursion turns into a chance for development and understanding. The family learns not exclusively to adjust to the interesting necessities of their youngster yet in addition to see the value in the variety of qualities that every part offers of real value.

In the midst of emergency, families frequently uncover stowed away gifts, foster new abilities, and find an aggregate limit with regards to development. The misfortune turns into an instructor, granting important illustrations about flexibility, diligence, and the boundless potential that arises when confronted with difficulties as a unified front.

The development catalyzed by difficulty isn't bound to individual individuals yet stretches out to the family in general. The common excursion of defeating difficulties turns into an account of aggregate development — an account of how a unified front can change misfortune into a chance for significant development and flexibility.

The Tradition of Aggregate Strength:

As families face and conquer difficulties together, they make a tradition of aggregate strength that reverberations through ages. The illustrations took in, the bonds fashioned, and the flexibility developed become a persevering through legacy passed down to future relatives. This heritage turns into a guide of motivation, reminding every age that, in solidarity, they have the solidarity to beat any misfortune.

Think about a family that, across ages, has confronted and vanquished monetary difficulties. The narratives of flexibility, cleverness, and the enduring help that relatives gave to each other become a piece of the family legend. This heritage imparts a feeling of certainty and solidarity in resulting ages, engaging them to stand up to difficulties with the information that they are essential for a genealogy set apart by aggregate strength.

The tradition of aggregate strength stretches out past the commonsense parts of confronting affliction. It turns into a social legacy — a bunch of values, customs, and stories that characterize the family's personality. These qualities, fashioned in the cauldron of difficulties, stress the significance of solidarity, common help, and the conviction that, together, the family can conquer any obstruction.

Chapter 7

"The Enduring Thread"

"The Getting through String"
In the mind boggling embroidery of human experience, the familial bond remains as a string that winds through the texture of our lives, sewing together snapshots of euphoria, challenges, and shared development. This getting through string, strong despite time and hardships, holds the actual embodiment of being a piece of a family. A string ties ages, rising above the limits of individual lifetimes and shaping a continuum of shared stories.

At the core of this getting through string is the idea of congruity — a consistent association that connects the past, present, and future. Families, as the vessels of this association, convey forward customs, values, and the aggregate insight amassed through ages. The persevering through string turns into a life saver, establishing people it might be said of having a place and giving an establishment whereupon personalities are molded.

One part of this persevering through string is the transmission of stories — the accounts that navigate time, conveying with them the reverberations of chuckling, the reverberation of shared difficulties, and the insight refined from lived encounters. These accounts, frequently went down through oral customs or set up accounts, become an indispensable piece of a family's character.

They are the strings that tight spot ages together, cultivating a feeling of coherence and shared legacy.

Consider the narrative of a family established in an unassuming community, where stories of versatility during monetary difficulties are passed down from grandparents to guardians and afterward to the more youthful individuals. The persevering through string in this story isn't simply the relating of difficulties yet the illustrations took in, the strength fashioned, and the aggregate soul that characterized the family's reaction to difficulty. As every age adds its section to the story, the string develops, consolidating new encounters while keeping an association with the past.

The getting through string is additionally unpredictably woven into the ceremonies and customs that families maintain. Whether it be the festival of social celebrations, yearly get-togethers, or the recognition of shared traditions, these practices become the join that tight spot relatives across time. The string of custom fills in as a consistent, a wellspring of solace and commonality that grounds people in their familial roots.

Consider a family that accumulates each late spring for a gathering, a practice maintained for ages. The persevering through string in this custom isn't simply the actual demonstration of meeting up however the immaterial bonds fortified every year — the giggling reverberating through the ages, the narratives told and retold, and the common feeling of having a place that rises above the progression of time. This custom turns into a demonstration of the persevering through nature of familial associations, framing a string that endures the mileage of evolving conditions.

The getting through string isn't resistant to the difficulties that life presents. It might confront strains, winds, and even snapshots of fraying. However, it is exactly in those minutes that the strength of the familial bond is uncovered. Families, as an aggregate unit, have the ability to repair the string, to wind around it back along with strings of figuring out, pardoning, and unrestricted love.

Consider a family wrestling with a time of friction, where conflicts and errors compromise the union of the getting through string. At such times, the strength of the familial bond is scrutinized. The eagerness to impart straightforwardly, to see each other's points of view, and to expand peace offerings of compromise turns into the needle that fastens the string once more into an embroidery of solidarity. It is an update that, even despite difficulties, the persevering through string has the ability to get by as well as to arise more grounded.

The getting through string is likewise communicated through the repeating idea of life altering situations. Births, relationships, and passings mark the progression of time, and the familial bond fills in as the consistent in the steadily evolving scene.

The string of life altering situations becomes entwined with the string of shared encounters, making a story that unfurls across ages.

Consider a family where the introduction of a kid turns into a pivotal event, for the quick guardians as well as for the whole more distant family. The persevering through string in this occasion is the aggregate euphoria, the common obligations, and the feeling of congruity as the infant turns into the most up to date expansion to the familial embroidered artwork. Likewise, in the midst of misfortune, the getting through string turns into a wellspring of comfort, giving a system to lamenting together and tracking down strength in the aggregate hug of shared recollections.

The getting through string is additionally apparent in the common qualities that families go down through the ages. These qualities, whether established in social practices, moral standards, or a common perspective, become the ethical compass that guides relatives through life's excursion. The transmission of values through the persevering through string is a conscious demonstration — a promise to safeguarding the quintessence of what the family holds dear.

Consider a family that puts a high worth on graciousness and liberality, characteristics imparted by grandparents and maintained by resulting ages. The persevering through string in this worth framework isn't simply the faith in being thoughtful yet the lived encounters that embody this standard. Demonstrations of liberality, empathy, and local area administration become the strings that wind through the family story, making an inheritance that stretches out past individual lifetimes.

The persevering through string is likewise appeared in the common hereditary qualities and characteristics that pass starting with one age then onto the next. The actual likenesses, character idiosyncrasies, and even gifts become strings that associate relatives across time. It is a string woven by the section of hereditary material, a many-sided design that mirrors the interconnectedness of familial connections.

Consider a family where imaginative gifts are gone down through ages — a grandma who was a talented painter, a parent with a skill for music, and a youngster who shows a characteristic energy for verse. The persevering through string in this imaginative genealogy isn't the ideal hereditary inclination however the common energy for inventive articulation. The family turns into a material where every part contributes their novel strokes, making a show-stopper that mirrors the creative heritage conveyed forward by the getting through string.

As families explore the intricacies of the advanced world, the persevering through string faces new difficulties. Globalization, changing cultural standards, and the requests of a quick moving life might bring erosions into the familial texture. In any case, it is unequivocally at these times of progress that the persevering through string has the valuable chance to develop, to consolidate new examples and adjust to the moving scene.

Consider a family adjusting to the computerized age, where virtual associations supplement actual social occasions. The persevering through string in this situation isn't simply the eye to eye collaborations yet the purposeful endeavors to keep a feeling of closeness across distances. Video calls, shared computerized spaces, and virtual festivals become the strings that span the actual holes, guaranteeing that the persevering through string stays versatile even with evolving conditions.

7.1 Reflection on the lasting impact of being a close-knit family.
Reflection on the Enduring Effect of Being an Affectionate Family

In the mosaic of human experience, the idea of family possesses a focal and persevering through place. An affectionate family, described areas of strength for by, shared encounters, and common help, makes a significant and enduring effect that stretches out a long ways past individual lifetimes. This reflection dives into the diverse elements of the enduring effect of being an affectionate family, investigating how the interconnectedness of familial connections shapes personality, strength, and a feeling of having a place.

Molding Character through Shared Accounts:

One of the getting through traditions of an affectionate family is its part in molding individual personalities. Family stories, customs, and values structure the account setting against which people characterize themselves. The common encounters inside the family become sections in the narrative of individual character, adding to a feeling of congruity and association.

Consider a family with a rich practice of narrating, where tales of versatility, wins, and shared chuckling are passed down from one age to another. The enduring effect of this narrating custom is clear in how every relative assimilates these stories as their very own piece character. The tales become a relating of the past as well as a wellspring of motivation, molding the qualities, convictions, and character of every person.

In an affectionate family, the molding of character is certainly not a single undertaking however a cooperative cycle. Relatives act as mirrors, reflecting back parts of oneself that could slip through the cracks in different settings. This aggregate mindfulness encourages a feeling of having a place and acknowledgment, permitting people to investigate and communicate their true selves inside the security net of familial securities.

Building Versatility through Aggregate Help:

The enduring effect of being an affectionate family is maybe most clear in the versatility that rises out of aggregate help. Life is unavoidably set apart by difficulties — wellbeing emergencies, monetary mishaps, or individual battles. In an affectionate family, the weight of these difficulties is shared, and flexibility turns into an aggregate undertaking.

Consider a family confronting the intricacies of a worldwide pandemic. The aggregate emotionally supportive network inside an affectionate family gives a cushion against the vulnerabilities and stresses that go with such occasions. The effect of this aggregate flexibility reaches out past the prompt test; it turns into a system for exploring future difficulties with a common strength that emerges from the interconnectedness of familial bonds.

In snapshots of emergency, the getting through help of an affectionate family fills in as an impetus for individual flexibility. The information that one isn't the only one to confront difficulties, yet rather a piece of a unified front, imparts a feeling of mental fortitude and assurance. The effect isn't only in conquering explicit misfortunes however in the development of a versatile outlook that can be drawn upon over the course of life's excursion.

Besides, the aggregate versatility of an affectionate family isn't bound to emergency reaction however penetrates regular day to day existence. The common consolation, festivity of accomplishments, and shared critical thinking establish a climate where people feel engaged to face challenges, seek after private objectives, and climate the unavoidable tempests of existence with a conviction that all is good that comes from being important for a strong unit.

Cultivating a Feeling of Having a place:

An affectionate family goes about as a cauldron for the improvement of a significant feeling of having a place. This sensation of being a necessary piece of a familial unit adds to a steady groundwork whereupon people can fabricate their lives. The effect of this feeling of having a place resonates through different parts of a singular's prosperity, forming mental, profound, and, surprisingly, actual wellbeing.

Think about the effect of an affectionate family on mental prosperity. The information that one is acknowledged and cherished genuinely inside the familial circle makes a mental anchor. This feeling of having a place decreases sensations of detachment and gives a protected base from which people can investigate the world, structure connections outside the family, and seek after self-awareness.

Inwardly, the effect of having a place with an affectionate family appears in the improvement of profound and significant associations. The common profound scene cultivates sympathy, empathy, and a comprehension of one another's weaknesses. These close to home bonds act as a wellspring of solace during troublesome times and uplift the delights experienced by and large.

Truly, the effect of an affectionate family on prosperity is obvious in the feeling of safety it gives. The information that there is a familial security net urges people to proceed with carefully thought out plans of action, realizing that they have an emotionally supportive network to return to if necessary. This feeling of safety adds to diminished feelings of anxiety, better by and large wellbeing, and a more noteworthy capacity to confront life's difficulties with versatility.

Impacting Relational Connections:

The enduring effect of being an affectionate family stretches out past the bounds of familial connections to impact how people draw in with the more extensive world. The relational abilities, correspondence styles, and values ingrained inside the familial unit frequently shape how people explore connections outside the family.

Think about an affectionate family that puts a high worth on successful correspondence and compromise. The effect of this relational intricacy is clear as people bring these relational abilities into their cooperations with companions, associates, and better halves. The capacity to listen effectively, communicate one's thoughts plainly, and explore clashes valuably turns into a learned way of behaving with sweeping ramifications.

Likewise, the qualities imparted inside an affectionate family, whether they be sympathy, participation, or a guarantee to local area administration, frequently become core values that people convey into their communications past the family circle. The effect is found in the development of significant companionships, fruitful coordinated efforts in proficient settings, and a feeling of social obligation that reaches out to the more extensive local area.

The enduring effect of an affectionate family on relational connections isn't simply in that frame of mind of explicit ways of behaving however in the basic qualities that shape these ways of behaving. The significance of trust, reliability, and common help becomes imbued, affecting how people construct and keep up with associations with others.

Developing Shared Recollections and Customs:

An affectionate family is an overseer of shared recollections and customs that make an embroidery of aggregate encounters. These common components add to the congruity of the familial story, making a feeling of legacy and heritage that perseveres across ages.

Think about a family with a practice of yearly get-aways, where each outing turns into a part in the family's story. The effect of these common recollections is significant — they act as anchor focuses in the family's aggregate history, making a feeling of congruity and giving a supply of valued encounters that tight spot relatives together.

Customs, whether they include special festivals, social ceremonies, or straight-forward day to day schedules, become strings in the persevering through texture of an affectionate family. The effect of these practices stretches out past the quick second; they act as markers of personality, making a feeling of union and having a place that people convey with them all through their lives.

The development of shared recollections and customs likewise fills in as a scaffold between ages. The effect is felt in the passing down of stories, the continuation of customs, and the protection of social practices.

This intergenerational trade turns into an unmistakable indication of the enduring effect of being an affectionate family, where the strings of custom are passed from one hand to another, winding around an embroidery that rises above time.

7.2 Consideration of the future and the legacy of intimacy.

Thought Representing things to come and the Tradition of Closeness

As families explore the flows of time, the thought representing things to come and the tradition of closeness becomes the overwhelming focus in the woven artwork of familial bonds. This consideration stretches out past quick worries to incorporate the more extensive effect of affectionate connections on the ages on the way. In investigating the tradition of closeness, we dive into the persevering through strings that interface past, present, and future, molding the story of a family's excursion and making a permanent imprint on the embroidery of human experience.

Planting Seeds for Future Associations:

One of the primary parts of considering the future inside an affectionate family is the purposeful development of associations that rise above ages. The seeds of future closeness are planted through the nature of connections sustained inside the nuclear family. Every collaboration, each common second, adds to the aggregate memory that will be passed down to people in the future.

Think about a family that puts accentuation on standard family get-togethers and reunions. The effect of these purposeful snapshots of harmony stretches out past the present, making a repository of shared encounters that will be treasured by relatives.

The tradition of closeness is implanted in the practices laid out today, giving a guide to people in the future to develop solid familial bonds.

The thought representing things to come includes a mindfulness that the connections constructed today will act as the establishment for the family's heritage. Thoughtful gestures, articulations of affection, and the fashioning of profound associations become the structure blocks of a familial legacy that perseveres across time. This tradition of closeness isn't simply a gift to the current age however an endowment to the individuals who will acquire the familial embroidery.

Passing Down Values and Customs:

The tradition of closeness reaches out past simple familial associations; it envelops the transmission of values and customs that structure the social character of a family. Thought for what's in store includes a conscious work to pass down these core values, guaranteeing that they become a compass for a long time into the future.

Values like sympathy, flexibility, and a promise to local area administration can be ingrained inside the family structure. The effect of these qualities isn't restricted to the present; they act as a directing power for future navigation, molding the personality of people who will convey the familial heritage forward.

Moreover, customs become an extension between ages, interfacing the past with what's in store. The effect of celebrating social celebrations, keeping up with family ceremonies, or maintaining explicit traditions is twofold — it saves the lavishness of familial history and gives people in the future a feeling of progression. The tradition of closeness is encapsulated in these getting through customs, filling in as a substantial articulation of shared personality.

Sustaining The capacity to appreciate people on a profound level:

Thought for the future inside an affectionate family includes a conscious spotlight on supporting capacity to understand individuals on a deeper level. The capacity to comprehend and deal with feelings, convey successfully, and construct significant connections turns into a critical part of the tradition of closeness. The capacity to understand people on a deeper level fills in as a legacy that prepares people to explore the intricacies of their own feelings and interface sympathetically with others.

The effect of encouraging capacity to appreciate people on a profound level inside the nuclear family stretches out a long ways past close connections. It adds to the production of genuinely strong people who are prepared to deal with the complexities of human associations. The tradition of closeness lies in the profound prosperity passed down to people in the future, making a family culture that values sympathy, open correspondence, and a profound comprehension of the human experience.

Consider a family that effectively takes part in discussions about feelings, energizes the statement of sentiments, and shows the significance of undivided attention. The effect of these purposeful endeavors is significant — it makes a heritage where people are receptive to their own feelings as well as skilled at building strong and sympathetic associations with others.

Cultivating Instructive and Self-awareness:

In taking into account the future, an affectionate family turns into a supporting climate for instructive and self-awareness. The effect of offering help for instructive pursuits, cultivating an adoration for learning, and empowering individual yearnings resonates across ages. The tradition of closeness is tracked down in the scholarly interest, strength, and self-viability imparted in relatives.

Think about a family that puts a top notch on schooling, where scholarly accomplishments are praised and a culture of constant learning is developed. The effect of this familial ethos stretches out into the future, affecting the profession decisions, self-improvement, and generally satisfaction of people inside the family. The tradition of closeness is reflected chasing information and self-improvement that turns into a principal quality of the family genealogy.

Besides, the support of individual yearnings inside an affectionate family adds to a tradition of independence and self-disclosure. The effect of supporting every relative in their one of a kind excursion is found in the variety of gifts, interests, and commitments that people bring to the aggregate familial story. The tradition of closeness lies in the opportunity conceded to people in the future to investigate their interests, pursue decisions lined up with their qualities, and cut out special ways inside the familial embroidered artwork.

Winding around a Tradition of Flexibility:

In considering the future, an affectionate family perceives the certainty of progress and the requirement for versatility. The effect of imparting a feeling of adaptability, flexibility, and receptiveness to change turns into a foundation of the tradition of closeness. This flexibility guarantees that the familial bonds major areas of strength for stay pertinent notwithstanding advancing conditions.

Consider a family that explores life's changes with a feeling of versatility — a movement, a lifelong change, or changes in relational peculiarities. The effect of these encounters, drew nearer with strength and a feeling of harmony, adds to the tradition of closeness. It sends a strong message to people in the future that the familial bonds are not unbending however unique, equipped for enduring change while holding their center strength.

The tradition of flexibility isn't just about answering outside transforms; it likewise includes embracing the developing personalities and yearnings of people inside the family. Thought for what's in store involves making a space where relatives feel upheld in investigating their developing selves, adjusting to new jobs, and adding to the family story in manners that mirror their genuine characters.

Protecting Social and Individual Narratives:

An affectionate family turns into a watchman of social and individual chronicles, saving stories that add to the tradition of closeness. The effect of recording family stories, keeping up with chronicles of photos, and passing down familial information is critical — it makes a continuum that interfaces the past, present, and future.

Consider a family that effectively takes part in discussions about its social legacy, shares stories about precursors, and praises the different foundations that add to the family's personality. The effect of these endeavors is clear in the protection of social lavishness, guaranteeing that people in the future acquire a familial heritage as well as a more extensive social embroidery.

Protecting individual narratives inside the family includes perceiving the meaning of individual excursions. Thought for what's to come involves making spaces for relatives to share their biographies, encounters, and examples learned. The effect of this training is significant — it cultivates a feeling of interconnectedness as people consider themselves to be important for a bigger story that traverses ages.

Developing a Tradition of Unrestricted Love:

At the core of the tradition of closeness is the development of unrestricted love inside an affectionate family. Thought for what's in store includes deliberately encouraging a climate where love isn't dependent upon accomplishments, similarity, or outer elements. The effect of unrestricted love is extraordinary — it makes a familial inheritance described by acknowledgment, support, and a profound close to home association.

Consider a family that communicates love uninhibitedly, celebrates individual uniqueness, and offers steady help during the two victories and hardships. The effect of this unqualified love is boundless — it turns into a heritage that penetrates the familial embroidery, impacting the manner in which people in the future methodology connections, explore difficulties, and express love consequently.

The tradition of unqualified love is likewise clear in how clashes are moved toward inside an affectionate family. Thought for what's in store includes showing compromise abilities, advancing absolution, and displaying sound correspondence. The effect of these practices is felt in the production of a heritage where clashes don't break connections however become open doors for development, understanding, and the reaffirmation of familial bonds.

7.3 Final thoughts on the enduring thread that weaves through generations.

Last Considerations on the Persevering through String that Winds Through Ages

In the complex dance of time, the getting through string of familial associations winds through the embroidery of ages, restricting the past, present, and future into a consistent story. As we ponder this persevering through string, it becomes clear that it is in excess of a simple similitude; it is a no nonsense substance that characterizes the embodiment of everyday life. In these last contemplations, we investigate the significant ramifications of the persevering through string and its immortal importance in forming the human experience across ages.

A Continuum of Shared Stories:

The persevering through string fills in as a continuum of shared accounts, a help that connects the tales of precursors with the encounters of relatives. A living chronicle conveys the giggling, tears, wins, and hardships of the individuals who preceded, permitting every age to add its novel part to the familial adventure. This continuum of shared stories is a demonstration of the wealth of human experience and the influence of narrating to rise above time.

Consider a family gathering where older folks recap stories of persistence during testing times, and the most youthful individuals enthusiastically ingest these accounts with wide-looked at wonder. The getting through string, in this specific circumstance, isn't simply an assortment of tales yet a scaffold that interfaces ages through the reverberation of shared encounters. It welcomes every relative to add to the continuous account, guaranteeing that the familial story is rarely stale however constantly developing with the rhythmic movement of time.

Establishes Previously, Arriving at Toward What's to come:

The getting through string, solidly established before, extends its rings toward the future, securing relatives one might say of progression and reason. It is an update that, as people explore the intricacies of current life, they are not uncontrolled in confinement but rather part of a more extensive story that traverses hundreds of years. This rootedness in the past turns into a wellspring of solidarity, giving an establishment whereupon future goals can be fabricated.

Think about a family with a well established custom of craftsmanship, where the abilities passed down starting with one age then onto the next become both a respect to the past and a signal directing future undertakings. The getting through string, in this unique circumstance, is the string of dominance — a pledge to greatness that has endured everyday hardship. It fills in as a suggestion to every relative that they are people with disengaged objectives as well as supporters of a heritage that stretches out past their nearby desires.

The string's scope toward what's in store is additionally apparent in how families plan for the future. Thought for the getting through string includes smart choices about schooling, vocation ways, and the transmission of values. The effect of these contemplations is significant — it shapes the direction of people in the future, guaranteeing that they acquire material abundance as well as the immaterial abundance of familial insight, values, and a feeling of direction.

An Embroidery of Strength:

Flexibility is woven into the actual texture of the persevering through string. It demonstrates the veracity of the hardships looked by precursors and, in doing as such, turns into a wellspring of motivation for confronting contemporary difficulties. The getting through string conveys the scars of misfortune yet additionally the victories of human soul, making an embroidery of versatility that sustains relatives against the tempests of life.

Consider a family that has endured monetary slumps, wellbeing emergencies, and individual misfortunes. The persevering through string, in this specific situation, is certainly not a delicate string that breaks under tension however a versatile line that ties relatives together even with difficulty. It fills in as an update that difficulties are not outlandish hindrances but rather open doors for development, learning, and the producing of more grounded familial bonds.

Besides, the embroidery of versatility stretches out past individual difficulties to aggregate reactions. The getting through string energizes an outlook of shared help, where relatives rally together during troublesome times. The effect of this aggregate versatility isn't simply in defeating prompt difficulties however in developing a common strength that turns into a persevering through heritage for people in the future to draw upon.

Interlaced Strings of Variety:

The persevering through string is certainly not a solid element; rather, it is contained interwoven strings of variety. It embraces the shifted encounters, points of view, and characters of every relative, making a mosaic of interconnected lives.

This variety isn't a wellspring of division yet a wellspring of solidarity, as every remarkable string adds to the energy and versatility of the familial embroidery.

Think about a family with individuals from various social foundations, where customs, dialects, and customs mix to make a rich embroidery of variety. The persevering through string, in this specific situation, is certainly not a solitary tint however a range of varieties that mirrors the magnificence of a mixed legacy. It fills in as an update that, in embracing variety, families not just honor the singular personalities of their individuals yet in addition add to a more extensive story of solidarity amidst contrasts.

The effect of entwined strings of variety is significant — it cultivates a feeling of consideration, acknowledgment, and shared regard inside the family. It turns into a heritage that people in the future acquire, empowering them to commend the uniqueness of every relative and to perceive the strength that emerges from embracing variety.

An Image of Whole Bonds:

At its center, the persevering through string is an image of whole bonds that continue in spite of the progression of time. It is a demonstration of the flexibility of familial associations, the strength of adoration, and the getting through nature of human connections. In snapshots of delight and distress, in the midst of festivity and reflection, the getting through string remains as a quiet observer to the resolute ties that tight spot relatives together.

Consider a family get-together where ages meet up to celebrate achievements, share stories, and reaffirm their associations. The persevering through string, in this specific situation, isn't simply a figurative idea yet a discernible reality that can be felt in the glow of embraces, the giggling that reverberations through shared spaces, and the aggregate recollections that are scratched into the hearts of every relative. It fills in as an image of whole bonds that rise above the impediments of existence.

The effect of this image reaches out past the prompt second — it turns into a wellspring of comfort during seasons of partition, an indication of shared history during snapshots of reflection, and an encouraging sign for people in the future. The persevering through string, as an image of solid bonds, is a reference point that enlightens the way ahead, empowering relatives to explore the excursion of existence with the information that they are essential for an option that could be more significant than themselves.